collections

Close Reader

GRADE 7

Program Consultants:

Kylene Beers

Martha Hougen

Carol Jago

William L. McBride

Erik Palmer

Lydia Stack

Cover, Title Page Photo Credits: ©Thomas Northcut/Getty Images

Printed in the U.S.A.

ISBN 978-0-544-09076-7

19 20 1468 20 19 18

4500707297 B C D E F G

COLLECTION 1
Bold Actions

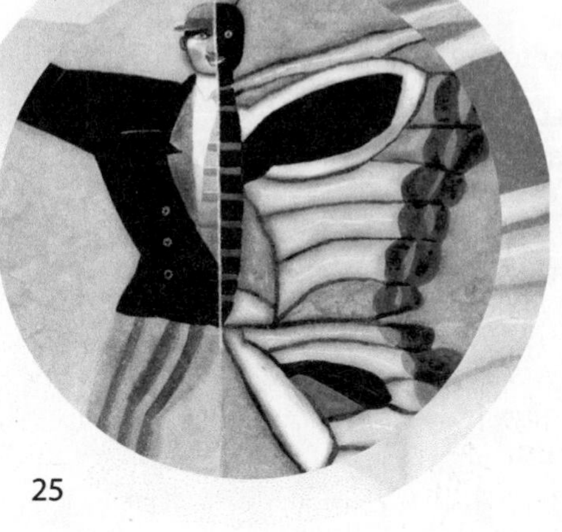

COLLECTION 2
Perception and Reality

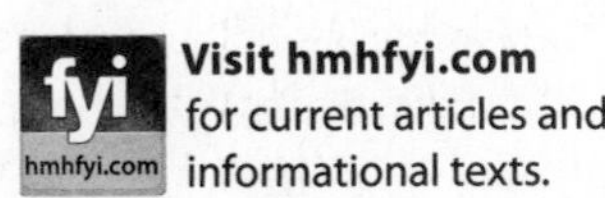

COLLECTION **3**
Nature at Work

COLLECTION **4**
Risk and Exploration

COLLECTION **5**

The Stuff of Consumer Culture

COLLECTION **6**

Guided by a Cause

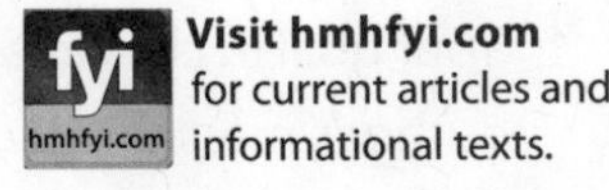

Visit hmhfyi.com for current articles and informational texts.

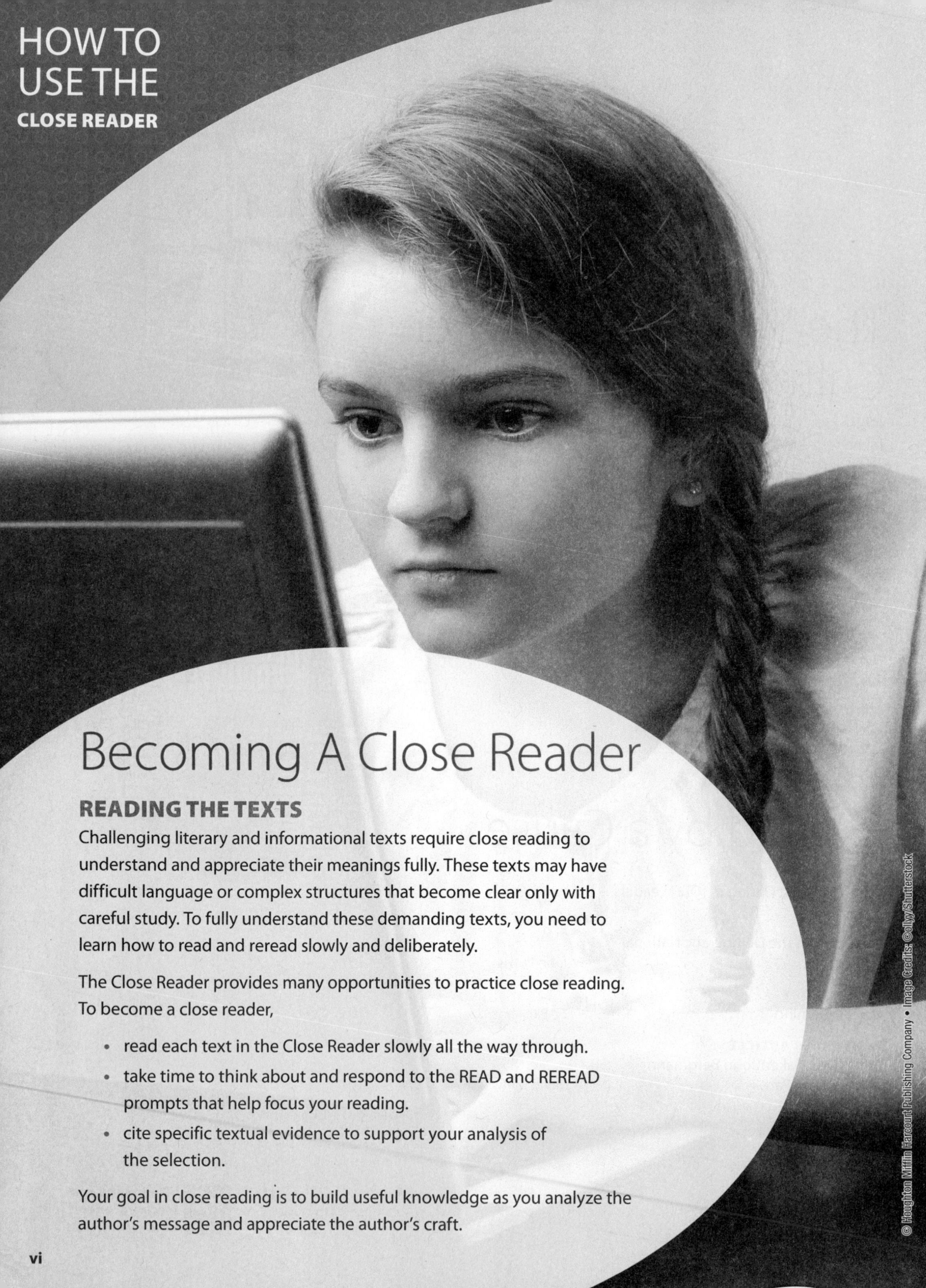

Becoming A Close Reader

READING THE TEXTS

Challenging literary and informational texts require close reading to understand and appreciate their meanings fully. These texts may have difficult language or complex structures that become clear only with careful study. To fully understand these demanding texts, you need to learn how to read and reread slowly and deliberately.

The Close Reader provides many opportunities to practice close reading. To become a close reader,

- read each text in the Close Reader slowly all the way through.
- take time to think about and respond to the READ and REREAD prompts that help focus your reading.
- cite specific textual evidence to support your analysis of the selection.

Your goal in close reading is to build useful knowledge as you analyze the author's message and appreciate the author's craft.

Background Eleanora E. Tate *was born in Canton, Missouri, and spent her first year of school in a one-room schoolhouse for students in the first through eighth grades. She wrote her first story when she was in the third grade. Tate says she writes books and stories so that all people can read about the proud history and culture of African Americans.*

Big Things Come in Small Packages

Short Story by Eleanora E. Tate

1. READ ▶ As you read lines 1–77, begin to collect and cite text evidence.
   - Underline details in lines 1–5 that describe the story's setting.
   - Circle several events that depend on the setting.
   - Circle the narrator's name and underline three things she reveals about herself and Tucker.

CLOSE READ Notes

I want to tell you about a boy I knew who lived in Morehead City, North Carolina, some years ago named Tucker Willis. He lived by Calico Creek where it narrows down to marsh grass, flounder, and fiddler crabs. It's not far from the back side of the Morehead City Port **Terminal,** where the big ships come in from the Atlantic Ocean.

Everybody liked him, and he was good at almost everything he put his hand to. But when Tucker turned eleven or twelve, he was still so short he looked like an elf. And you know how it is when you're a little different from other folks in even some harmless kind of way. Kids called him Tom Thumb, squirt, midget, inchworm, dwarf.

I thought Tucker was the cutest little thing in the world. But to him back then I was ole knock-kneed LaShana Mae, the girl who lived down the street. I was a couple years younger than him. We were friends, though, and went to the same church—St. Luke's Missionary Baptist—and the same school.

People tease him for being small, and he does not like it.

terminal: end of a transportation line

3

Background

This paragraph provides information about the text you are about to read. It helps you understand the context of the selection through additional information about the author, the subject, or the time period in which the text was written.

READ ▶

With practice, you can learn how to be a close reader. Questions and specific instructions at the beginning of the selection and on the bottom of the pages will guide your close reading of each text.

These questions and instructions

- refer to specific sections of the text.
- ask you to look for and mark up specific information in the text.
- prompt you to record inferences and text analysis in the side margins.
- help you begin to collect and cite text evidence.

CLOSE READ Notes

That's how I'd see Tucker surfing. He even got teased about surfing, because not many black kids we knew surfed. Shoot, as much as we all loved the water, not a whole lot of us even knew how to swim. I didn't. Not until Tucker taught me later on.

He and his dad or mom would fish out on their own little pier all night sometimes with a Coleman lantern[1] for light. His folks used regular rods and reels. I never fished out there at night with them because the mosquitoes and the gnats would about eat me up.

Plus, my momma liked to tell me that they used to do baptizing in that creek, which was okay. But then Momma'd say, "LaShana Mae, you watch out about being around that creek by yourself at night. The people who got baptized there and who've passed on come back to that creek as spirits in the middle of the night when the moon's full. They'll be singing and celebrating and shouting and praising, and they don't want to be **disturbed.** Unless you wanna join in with 'em."

Me being a scared little kid, you can believe that Momma didn't have to worry about me going out to *nobody's* Calico Creek by myself at night. But sometimes I'd go to my window at night and look out to see if anybody was celebrating the way she said. All I ever saw were grown folks fishing. Sometimes somebody would holler when they caught a big one. After I got grown I understood that Momma told me that story to try to help me stay out of trouble. She was worried I'd drown or get into some kind of foolishness. Well, it worked. I knew that it was easy to get into trouble when you're out someplace where you're not supposed to be.

disturbed:

[1] **Coleman lantern:** a lamp that burns pressurized kerosene to give light.

2. ◀ REREAD Reread lines 6–26. In the margin, describe the conflict Tucker faces. Circle the text that foreshadows a future event.

3. READ ▶ As you read lines 78–116, continue to cite textual evidence.
   - Circle text that creates suspense about a major event in the plot that will take place.
   - Underline text that suggests that his meeting with Richard was important to Tucker.
   - In the margin, make an inference about Tucker's attitude toward Richard.

5

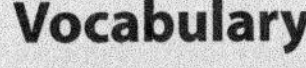

Vocabulary

Critical vocabulary words appear in the margin throughout most selections. Consult a print or online dictionary to define the word on your own.

When you see a vocabulary word in the margin,

- write the definition of each word in the margin.
- be sure your definition fits the context of the word as it is used in the text.
- check your definition by substituting it in place of the vocabulary word from the text. Your definition should make sense in the context of the selection.

◀ REREAD

To further guide your close reading, REREAD questions at the bottom of the page will

- ask you to focus on a close analysis of a smaller chunk of text.
- prompt you to analyze literary elements and devices, as well as the meaning and structure of informational text.
- help you go back into the text and "read between the lines" to uncover meanings and central ideas.

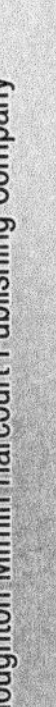

CLOSE READ Notes

There really was a man named Richard Etheridge, a professional fisherman who was born in 1844 on Roanoke Island off North Carolina. A member of the Thirty-sixth U.S. Colored Troops of the Union Army, he fought at the Battle of New Market Heights in Virginia during the Civil War. And in 1880, Etheridge was hired as the Keeper of the Pea Island Lifesaving Station on the Barrier Islands (the Outer Banks) of North Carolina. The station continued to set a high standard of performance with its all-black personnel until 1947, when the Coast Guard closed down the facilities.

posthumously:

No one made any formal recognition of the Pea Island surfmen's daring sea rescues until 1996. In March of that year, Etheridge and his men were finally acknowledged ***posthumously*** *in formal ceremonies in Washington, D.C., with a Gold Lifesaving Medal from the United States Coast Guard. Etheridge and his wife and daughter are buried on the grounds of the North Carolina Aquarium in Manteo, which maintains an exhibit on these brave men.*

9. REREAD AND DISCUSS Reread lines 260–275. With a partner, discuss the inclusion of the historical facts at the end of a fictional story. Does it add anything to the story or is it unnecessary?

SHORT RESPONSE

Cite Text Evidence Was Tucker the hero that everyone thought him to be, or was Richard mostly responsible for the rescue? **Cite text evidence** to support your opinion.

REREAD AND DISCUSS

These prompts encourage you to work with a partner or in a small group to discuss specific events, details, statements, and evidence from the text. These discussions will allow you to acquire and share knowledge about the texts you are reading.

As you engage in these discussions,

- be sure to cite specific text evidence in support of your statements.
- pose questions and integrate your ideas with the ideas of others.
- collaborate to reach a consensus or call attention to evidence that might have been missed or misinterpreted.
- acknowledge the views of others and be ready to modify your own thinking.

SHORT RESPONSE

At the end of each text, you will have an opportunity to sum up your thinking by completing a Short Response. The Short Response represents a place to convey some of the ideas you have developed through close reading of the text.

When you write your Short Response,

- review all of your margin notes and REREAD answers.
- circle or highlight evidence from your notes that supports your position or point of view.
- clearly state your point of view and support it with reasons.
- cite specific text evidence to support your reasons.

COLLECTION 1

Bold Actions

COLLECTION 1

Bold Actions

"Be bold, take courage . . . and be strong of soul."

—Ovid

Background Eleanora E. Tate *was born in Canton, Missouri, and spent her first year of school in a one-room schoolhouse for students in the first through eighth grades. She wrote her first story when she was in the third grade. Tate says she writes books and stories so that all people can read about the proud history and culture of African Americans.*

Big Things Come in Small Packages

Short Story by Eleanora E. Tate

1. **READ ▶** As you read lines 1–77, begin to collect and cite text evidence.
   - Underline details in lines 1–5 that describe the story's setting.
   - Circle several events that depend on the setting.
   - Circle the narrator's name and underline three things she reveals about herself and Tucker.

I want to tell you about a boy I knew who lived in Morehead City, North Carolina, some years ago named Tucker Willis. He lived by Calico Creek where it narrows down to marsh grass, flounder, and fiddler crabs. It's not far from the back side of the Morehead City Port **Terminal,** where the big ships come in from the Atlantic Ocean.

terminal:

Everybody liked him, and he was good at almost everything he put his hand to. But when Tucker turned eleven or twelve, he was still so short he looked like an elf. And you know how it is when you're a little different from other folks in even some harmless kind of way. Kids called him Tom Thumb, squirt, midget, inchworm, dwarf.

I thought Tucker was the cutest little thing in the world. But to him back then I was ole knock-kneed LaShana Mae, the girl who lived down the street. I was a couple years younger than him. We were friends, though, and went to the same church—St. Luke's Missionary Baptist—and the same school.

Back in those days, in the 1970s, young boys and girls didn't hang out as boyfriend and girlfriend like kids do now. Plus, I was just a skinny girl with braids and braces. Kids called me Wires because of those braces, and boy, did it ever make me mad! So Tucker and I had a lot in common, and lots of times we talked about the things kids called us, especially when we went fishing.

Even though being called those names hurt, Tucker gave up fighting the kids who said them. Fighting didn't help. The name-callers were all too big for him to beat up. So after a while, he learned to ignore the teasing. Most times he laughed it off. He was a tough little dude. But oh mercy, how he hated those names!

One day Tucker did something that made everybody stop calling him names he didn't like. I think it helped him grow a few inches, too.

You need to know a few things about this boy before I tell you what changed things around. Tucker could do almost anything that any other kid his age could do. He was a hotshot shortstop on the Little League baseball team. He could jump like a flea on the basketball court. He was smart in school. He was in the Boy Scouts. He could swim like a fish—and even surf!

He looked like a Tootsie Roll to me in that big ocean. Yeah, I had a name for him, too. I called him Tootsie Roll, but never to his face. I just kept it to myself. And when I called him that in my head, I didn't mean it in a bad way.

pier:

Tucker could do some fishing. He especially liked to fish his folks' little **pier** alongside their house. In the summertime he'd lie on his stomach on the pier and catch some of the biggest flounder to come out of Calico Creek. Instead of a rod and reel, he used a handful of fishing line, a hook baited with shrimp, and a sinker to keep the bait from floating on the surface.

He'd dangle that shrimp an inch or two off the bottom, right in front of a flounder's nose. Sometimes we'd fish together on his pier, and I wouldn't catch diddlysquat, not even a pinfish, not even a lizard fish, nothing. But ole Tootsie Roll could catch 'em.

I tried fishing the way he did, but most of the time I used a rod and reel 'cause I thought the way Tucker did it was country. I still couldn't catch anything, not in Calico Creek. I did all right when I fished at the pier in Atlantic Beach.

That's how I'd see Tucker surfing. He even got teased about surfing, because not many black kids we knew surfed. Shoot, as much as we all loved the water, not a whole lot of us even knew how to swim. I didn't. Not until Tucker taught me later on.

He and his dad or mom would fish out on their own little pier all night sometimes with a Coleman lantern[1] for light. His folks used regular rods and reels. I never fished out there at night with them because the mosquitoes and the gnats would about eat me up.

Plus, my momma liked to tell me that they used to do baptizing in that creek, which was okay. But then Momma'd say, "LaShana Mae, you watch out about being around that creek by yourself at night. The people who got baptized there and who've passed on come back to that creek as spirits in the middle of the night when the moon's full. They'll be singing and celebrating and shouting and praising, and they don't want to be **disturbed.** Unless you wanna join in with 'em."

disturbed:

Me being a scared little kid, you can believe that Momma didn't have to worry about me going out to *nobody's* Calico Creek by myself at night. But sometimes I'd go to my window at night and look out to see if anybody was celebrating the way she said. All I ever saw were grown folks fishing. Sometimes somebody would holler when they caught a big one. After I got grown I understood that Momma told me that story to try to help me stay out of trouble. She was worried I'd drown or get into some kind of foolishness. Well, it worked. I knew that it was easy to get into trouble when you're out someplace where you're not supposed to be.

[1] **Coleman lantern:** a lamp that burns pressurized kerosene to give light.

2. REREAD Reread lines 6–26. In the margin, describe the conflict Tucker faces. Circle the text that foreshadows a future event.

3. READ As you read lines 78–116, continue to cite textual evidence.
   - Circle text that creates suspense about a major event in the plot that will take place.
   - Underline text that suggests that his meeting with Richard was important to Tucker.
   - In the margin, make an inference about Tucker's attitude toward Richard.

Anyway, what happened to change all the name-calling started when Tucker was on his pier trying to catch a flounder. He noticed a man standing on the Moten Motel dock just a few yards from him. The man had a thick white mustache and Vandyke beard and wore a blue-and-gold military-style jacket and cap. I wasn't there, so I didn't see him, but that's what Tucker told me.

When the man waved, Tucker, being a friendly kind of kid, waved back. They struck up a conversation. The man said his name was Richard and that he was staying at the motel for a few days. His home was in Manteo, on Roanoke Island, not far from the Outer Banks, where he worked with the U.S. Lifesaving Service.

Tucker figured what he meant was that he was with the U.S. Coast Guard. Tucker was pretty knowledgeable about the coast guard, but he had never heard of this lifesaving service. Tucker asked the man if he liked to fish. Richard said yes. He'd been a commercial fisherman before he became a captain in the lifesaving service. As a lifesaver, he said, he and his men went into the ocean in the middle of hurricanes and nor'easters[2] to save passengers and crew members whose ships were sinking.

Of course, anything about water fascinated Tucker, so he must have asked this Richard a million questions. Richard didn't seem to mind, though. He said he didn't get to talk to kids much anymore.

Richard said a good crewman had to be strong, an excellent swimmer, a quick thinker, and in good physical health, have good eyesight, and understand how dangerous the sea can be. He told so many stories about lifesaving that Tucker wished he could enlist right away, and said so. He had the right **qualifications**—other than being too young, of course. And too short.

qualifications:

Richard told him it wasn't the size of a person that got the job done. It was how bad the person wanted to do it. How were those huge ships two and more stories high able to move into the Morehead City port and back out to sea? Most couldn't do it without little tugboats pushing and pulling them in, Richard said. A tugboat could bring in a ship many times its size.

Richard said that Tucker would make a good tugboat and one day might even grow to be a big ship. He thanked Tucker for the conversation, said maybe they'd meet again, and then the man

[2] **nor'easters:** storms with winds blowing from the northeast.

wandered off back toward the motel. Tucker said for the rest of the afternoon, he thought over what Richard had said.

A few days later, Tucker decided to go with his dad to the Atlantic Beach pier to fish. His daddy worked there as a cook. For some reason I couldn't go that day. I've always wished I had. Tucker said he took his surfboard too, in case fishing got slow. It was early morning, but a hot July wind blew in from the southwest, making the waves choppy and sandy. The tide was going out. Hardly anybody was on the pier, which was another hint that the fish might not be biting. Tucker said only one guy was in the water, floating on a red raft like a huge jellyfish.

After a good hour had passed and he hadn't got a bite, Tucker left his rod and reel with his father in the pier restaurant's kitchen and went surfing. After he swam out far enough, he climbed onto his surfboard and rode a wave in. When he glanced back at the pier, guess who he saw? His new friend, Richard, on the pier, clapping for him. At least this time he had on shorts and a regular shirt. Tucker said he bet Richard had about burnt up in that heavy uniform the other day.

Richard hollered, "Do it, Tugboat! Pull that ole wave in!"

Tugboat? Tucker said he frowned until he remembered Richard's story about tugboats. So he waved back and swam out to pull in another one, passing the man on the raft. The man said, "You're

4. **◀ REREAD** Reread lines 100–116. Explain the significance of Richard's statement that "Tucker would make a good tugboat and one day might even grow to be a big ship." Cite specific text evidence to support your explanation.

5. **READ ▶** As you read lines 117–183, continue to cite textual evidence.

- In the margin, take notes about how suspense is built in this section.
- Circle the paragraph that is most likely the story's climax.

> **"He thrashed around in the water screaming that he couldn't swim."**

kinda little to be way out here, ain't ya, squirt?" Tucker just shook his head and kept going.

Tucker pulled in four more waves until he noticed a tall purple thunderhead rising up on the southwest horizon. That cloud meant a storm was probably on its way, but Tucker figured he had at least half an hour before the wind kicked up the waves and blew the cloud in and the rain began. Tucker wasn't afraid of a thing, but his common sense and his folks had told him to always leave away from water when storms and lightning came along. It's hard to get grown without having common sense, because being stupid can get you killed sometimes.

Keeping an eye on the horizon, Tucker went on pulling in those waves until a huge one arched up behind his back and crashed down on him. Tucker disappeared.

Wipeout. No big deal for Tucker, though. He popped right up in the water and grabbed his board, which was tied to his ankle. He was all right. But the man on the raft wasn't. He thrashed around in the water screaming that he couldn't swim.

As that big black cloud spread across the sky toward them, the wind and waves grew rougher. Wanting to help the man, but concerned about his own safety, Tucker hesitated, then straddled his surfboard and, using his hands for oars, paddled toward the raft. He'd have time to get the guy's raft back to him and then head in. But as Tucker passed, the man lunged at the surfboard, knocking Tucker off.

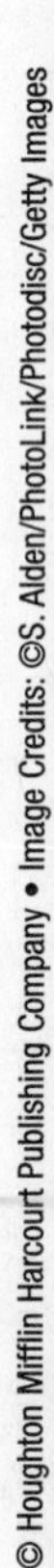

And then this guy grabbed hold of Tucker! Wrapped up in that big bear's arms and legs, with the sea getting choppier, Tucker said he knew he was about to die. He began to pray.

But something lifted Tucker up through the water and onto his surfboard, where he was able to catch his breath. That's when he saw his friend Richard in the water, too! Have mercy! Richard was hauling that raft toward the man. With two big heaves, Richard snatched that guy straight up out of the water and onto the raft.

Richard yelled, "Let's push and pull it, Tugboat! Push and pull it in!"

Somehow Tucker and Richard pushed and pulled that raft—with the guy glued to it—close enough to shore that the man was able to wade in the rest of the way. Four or five people splashed into the water and helped them onto the beach and into the pier house. One of the helpers was a reporter on vacation.

As soon as everybody was inside the pier house, the rain poured down. An arrow of lightning whizzed across the pier into the water and lit up the whole ocean. That's when Tucker said he got scared, seeing that lightning. He'd have been fried alive, you know. The guy Tucker rescued was named Nibbles. Mr. Nibbles was so grateful that he gave Tucker a hundred dollars right on the spot.

The reporter interviewed everybody and took pictures of Tucker, Nibbles, and Tucker's dad, who almost had a heart attack when he heard what happened. When the reporter asked how such a small boy was able to rescue a big, grown man, Tucker said, "'Cause I'm a tugboat, like Richard said. We pull the big ones in."

But when Tucker turned around to point out Richard, he couldn't find him.

6. **REREAD AND DISCUSS** Reread lines 140–148. With a partner, discuss the details that build suspense. What do you think these details foreshadow? Support your answer with explicit textual evidence.

7. **READ** As you read lines 184–237, continue to cite textual evidence.

- In the margin, explain how Tucker's conflict is resolved.
- Then, summarize what Tucker learns about Richard in lines 216–237.

The reporter's story about Tucker's rescue was in the local paper, then got picked up by the Associated Press and went all over the world. CBS TV even flew him and his folks to New York to be on its morning show. Afterwards, back home in Morehead City, strangers stopped Tucker on the street, in stores, even came to his home. They wanted to see the little "tugboat" that hauled in that big man, and get his autograph.

Businesses up and down Arendell Street put up WELCOME HOME, TUGBOAT! posters in their windows. And there was a parade. Tucker was a hero! He and the mayor rode on the back of a big ole white Cadillac convertible and waved at everybody. I was so proud that I almost forgot and hollered out, "Way to go, Tootsie Roll!" but I caught myself in time.

Everybody—even local folks—called Tucker Tugboat after that, including us kids. We'd never seen a real live hero close up before, especially one our age. It wasn't cool anymore to tease him with those other names. Funny how things can turn right around, isn't it?

And you know what? Tucker grew to be six feet five. He played on the North Carolina Central University Eagles basketball team, joined the U.S. Coast Guard, and lives in Kill Devil Hills, North Carolina, on the Outer Banks.

But there's something Tucker never figured out. When he first told people that Richard was the real hero, nobody believed him. Apparently nobody but Tucker had seen Richard—not even Mr. Nibbles.

There's more. When Tucker went into the pier gift shop to spend some of his rescue money, he picked up a book about the coast guard. He was thumbing through it when he stopped at an old-timey picture of some black men wearing jackets like Richard's. They were standing in front of a building on the Outer Banks. Below it was a picture of—yes, Richard! Mustache, beard, jacket, everything!

Tucker read, "History of the Pea Island Lifesaving Service. Captain Richard Etheridge was Keeper of the Pea Island Lifesaving Service, a forerunner of part of what is now the U.S. Coast Guard. This unique, all African American, courageous lifesaving crew, and those who followed, saved hundreds of shipwrecked passengers' lives by plunging into the stormy seas and bringing their charges back to safety."

Tucker said he shot out of that gift shop toward the restaurant to show his dad the book to prove his case, but what he read next made him stop: "Captain Etheridge, born in 1844 on Roanoke Island in North Carolina, died in 1900."

Tucker said he read that date fifteen or twenty times before it started to sink in. Nineteen hundred? Richard Etheridge had been dead for almost one hundred years. How was it possible a dead man helped him save that guy? Unless Richard was a ghost. He'd been talking to, and swimming with—a ghost?

You can believe Tucker hit up the library that very next day and searched for as much information as he could find on Richard Etheridge. There wasn't much, but what he read was that Richard Etheridge was all those great things he had read about and that he still died in 1900.

A few years later, when Tucker's folks visited the North Carolina Aquarium on Roanoke Island, Tucker found Richard Etheridge's grave and monument. Etheridge's headstone was marked 1844–1900. That's when Tucker stopped talking about Richard being involved in the rescue. Unless somebody asked.

So now, if you run into Tucker "Tugboat" Willis, ask him about the rescue, and he'll tell you. Then, real carefully, ask if he ever met Richard Etheridge. He'll tell you yes, he did, and what he learned. What he learned was that it pays to be polite to everybody you meet, like Tucker was to a man named Richard. You never know when that person might help you.

And every time Tucker tells me the story, he tells it to me the same way I told it to you. Seeing how Tucker turned out proves that some mighty things that help folks out in some mighty big ways can come in some mighty small packages.

It also proves that good things come to those who wait, like I did. I know, because I'm Mrs. LaShana Mae Willis, Tugboat's wife.

8. **READ ▶** As you read lines 238–275, continue to cite textual evidence.

- Underline the reason Tucker stops talking about Richard's involvement in the rescue (lines 243–247).
- Circle what you learn about the narrator.

There really was a man named Richard Etheridge, a professional fisherman who was born in 1844 on Roanoke Island off North Carolina. A member of the Thirty-sixth U.S. Colored Troops of the Union Army, he fought at the Battle of New Market Heights in Virginia during the Civil War. And in 1880, Etheridge was hired as the Keeper of the Pea Island Lifesaving Station on the Barrier Islands (the Outer Banks) of North Carolina. The station continued to set a high standard of performance with its all-black personnel until 1947, when the Coast Guard closed down the facilities.

No one made any formal recognition of the Pea Island surfmen's daring sea rescues until 1996. In March of that year, Etheridge and his men were finally acknowledged ***posthumously*** *in formal ceremonies in Washington, D.C., with a Gold Lifesaving Medal from the United States Coast Guard. Etheridge and his wife and daughter are buried on the grounds of the North Carolina Aquarium in Manteo, which maintains an exhibit on these brave men.*

posthumously:

9. **REREAD AND DISCUSS** Reread lines 260–275. With a partner, discuss the inclusion of the historical facts at the end of a fictional story. Does it add anything to the story or is it unnecessary?

SHORT RESPONSE

Cite Text Evidence Was Tucker the hero that everyone thought him to be, or was Richard mostly responsible for the rescue? **Cite text evidence** to support your opinion.

Background *At approximately 29,000 feet above sea level, Mount Everest is the highest mountain in the world. More than five thousand people have reached the summit of Mount Everest since the first successful climb in 1953 by Edmund Hillary and Tenzing Norgay. However, the climb is extremely dangerous; more than 200 people have died attempting to reach the top.*

Finding Your Everest

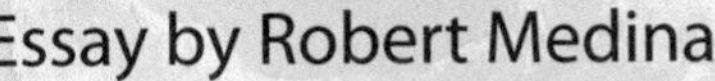

Essay by Robert Medina

CLOSE READ Notes

1. **READ ▶** As you read lines 1–33, begin to collect and cite text evidence.
   - Circle the most important information you learn about Jordan Romero in lines 1–13.
   - Explain in the margin what is meant by "the seven summits."
   - Underline details in lines 22–33 that explain what Jordan achieved.

Can parents go too far in supporting their children's dreams? This is a question people sometimes ask when they hear the story of the teenage mountain climber, Jordan Romero. Between the ages of 10 and 15, Jordan climbed the highest mountain on every continent—and his father and stepmother climbed them with him. They call themselves Team Jordan.

Paul Romero, Jordan's father, was taken by surprise when his 9-year-old son firmly announced his intention to climb "the seven summits." Jordan had seen a mural at school, showing the seven peaks that make up this **pantheon** of mountains. When he told his father what he wanted to do, Paul Romero's jaw dropped. Paul Romero is an experienced mountaineer, so he knew what was involved. He also knew his son.

pantheon:

“We’ve always taught him to just think big and we’ll try to make it happen,” Paul Romero said. But, as Romero later noted, there was a fine line between encouraging his son and pushing him too far. The father began by training his son so that he could “begin to even understand what mountaineering was—that there’s this long, hard, dirty, un-fun hours and days and weeks of carrying packs and long, extensive, brutal travel, and all this type of stuff just before you can even think of climbing a mountain.”

persevered:

Jordan **persevered**, though, and in July 2006, when he was 10 years old, Jordan and his family climbed 19,300-foot-high Mount Kilimanjaro, the highest peak on the African continent. This was the first rung in the amazing ladder that Jordan Romero had set out to climb. Over the next five and a half years, Team Jordan climbed Mount Elbrus in Russia (2007), Mount Aconcagua in South America (2007), Mount McKinley in North America (2008), Mount Carstensz Pyramid in Indonesia (2009), Mount Everest in Asia (2010), and Vinson Massif in Antarctica (2011). In many of these climbs, Jordan set a world record as the youngest ever to climb the peak. When he completed the seven summits at 15, he was the youngest person ever to accomplish that feat.

controversy:

It was the Mount Everest ascent—when Jordan was only 13 years old—that has created the greatest **controversy.** Jordan’s feat as the youngest person to reach “the top of the world” was publicized

2. REREAD Reread lines 14–21. In the margin, restate in your own words what Paul Romero says about mountaineering.

3. READ As you read lines 34–52, continue to cite textual evidence.

- Underline the medical claim (a position or opinion) about the dangers of mountain climbing to a 13-year-old.
- Circle the medical claim that offers a counterargument, or response, to the dangers of mountain climbing to a 13-year-old.
- Underline the opinion given by another mountain climber.

around the world. "How Young Is Too Young?" asked one newspaper headline. Many mountain climbers and medical experts questioned whether a 13-year-old boy could climb so high (Mount Everest is almost 30,000 feet high) without physically harming his body. Dr. Michael Bradley, a psychologist and expert on teen behavior, noted, "Most 13-year-olds don't have the wiring to make **cognitive** life-and-death decisions and are not truly able to understand what they're signing on for." Another physician, Dr. Peter Hackett, reported that there are conflicting opinions about the effects on a young brain. Some theories say that a young brain is more resilient; others say that it may be more vulnerable.

cognitive:

Many climbers take exception to the publicity surrounding Team Jordan. Everest climber Todd Burleson summed it up by saying, "He's got his whole life to climb Everest. Being the youngest boy to climb is a fashionable, celebrity-oriented sort of thing. But it's not about the mountains. It's like trying to get your PhD at ten."

Paul Romero claims that he is fully aware of the risks. There is a fine line between encouraging Jordan and pushing him too far, he says. He talked about the point where Jordan might have "reached his maximum mentally, physically, and where the risk has become too high." He said, "Jordan has just not even come close to that point yet."

And what about Jordan, now that he has accomplished his goal of climbing the seven summits before his 16th birthday? Unsurprisingly,

4. **REREAD AND DISCUSS** Reread lines 49–52. With a small group, discuss whether the evidence Todd Burleson cites is sufficient to support his opinion that Jordan and his family are just publicity seekers.

5. **READ** As you read lines 53–68, continue to cite textual evidence.
   - In the margin, restate the claim that Paul Romero makes in lines 53–57.
   - Circle the main idea in lines 58–65.
   - Underline the details that support the main idea.

he has a new mission. He calls it Find Your Everest. In 2012 Team Jordan set out to encourage young people to be active and healthy and to pursue their own adventures. In the process, he is inviting young people to join him in climbing the highest peak in each state. (They range from Denali or Mount McKinley at 20,320 feet to Florida's greatest height—345-foot-high Britton Hill!)

"I feel good about what my parents have taught me about setting goals," Jordan says. And now he wants to spread that message to others.

6. **REREAD** Reread lines 58–68. Make a note in the margin about how people might react to Jordan's new mission, considering the response to his earlier climbs.

SHORT RESPONSE

Cite Text Evidence The article opens with the question, "Can parents go too far in supporting their children's dreams?" Review your reading notes, and answer the question as it relates to the Romeros, evaluating the strength of the claims offered. Be sure to **cite text evidence** in your response.

Background *Many Greek myths are about characters who stray beyond the limits set by Greek gods and goddesses or who ignore their warnings. In this myth, Arachne (ə-răk′nē), a weaver, pits herself against Athene (ə-thē′nē), the goddess of wisdom and all crafts, particularly weaving.*

Arachne

Greek Myth retold by Olivia E. Coolidge

1. **READ ▶** As you read lines 1–37, begin to collect and cite text evidence.
   - Underline details that describe Arachne's skill.
   - Circle details that reveal Arachne's personality.

Arachne was a maiden who became famous throughout Greece, though she was neither wellborn nor beautiful and came from no great city. She lived in an **obscure** little village, and her father was a humble dyer of wool. In this he was very skillful, producing many varied shades, while above all he was famous for the clear, bright scarlet which is made from shellfish, and which was the most glorious of all the colors used in ancient Greece. Even more skillful than her father was Arachne. It was her task to spin the fleecy wool into a fine, soft thread and to weave it into cloth on the high-standing loom[1] within the cottage. Arachne was small and pale from much working. Her eyes were light and her hair was a dusty brown, yet she was quick and graceful, and her fingers, roughened as they were, went so fast that it was hard to follow their flickering movements. So soft and even

obscure:

[1] **high-standing loom:** a tall frame used to hold threads in a vertical position as other threads are woven through horizontally.

was her thread, so fine her cloth, so gorgeous her embroidery, that soon her products were known all over Greece. No one had ever seen the like of them before.

At last Arachne's fame became so great that people used to come from far and wide to watch her working. Even the graceful nymphs would steal in from stream or forest and peep shyly through the dark doorway, watching in wonder the white arms of Arachne as she stood at the loom and threw the shuttle[2] from hand to hand between the hanging threads, or drew out the long wool, fine as a hair, from the distaff[3] as she sat spinning. "Surely Athene herself must have taught her," people would murmur to one another. "Who else could know the secret of such marvelous skill?"

indignantly:

Arachne was used to being wondered at, and she was immensely proud of the skill that had brought so many to look on her. Praise was all she lived for, and it displeased her greatly that people should think anyone, even a goddess, could teach her anything. Therefore when she heard them murmur, she would stop her work and turn round **indignantly** to say, "With my own ten fingers I gained this skill, and by hard practice from early morning till night. I never had time to stand looking as you people do while another maiden worked. Nor if I had, would I give Athene credit because the girl was more skillful than I. As for Athene's weaving, how could there be finer cloth or

[2] **shuttle:** a piece of wood holding the thread that is to be woven horizontally through the vertical threads on a loom.

[3] **distaff:** a short rod for holding wool that is to be spun into a thread.

2. REREAD Reread lines 26–37. Explain why Arachne is so indignant. What character traits does Arachne reveal with this behavior? Support your answer with explicit textual evidence.

3. READ As you read lines 38–67, continue to cite textual evidence.

- Underline the advice the old woman gives Arachne.
- In the margin, restate Arachne's response to the woman's advice.
- In the margin, describe Arachne's reaction when she finds out she's speaking to Athene.

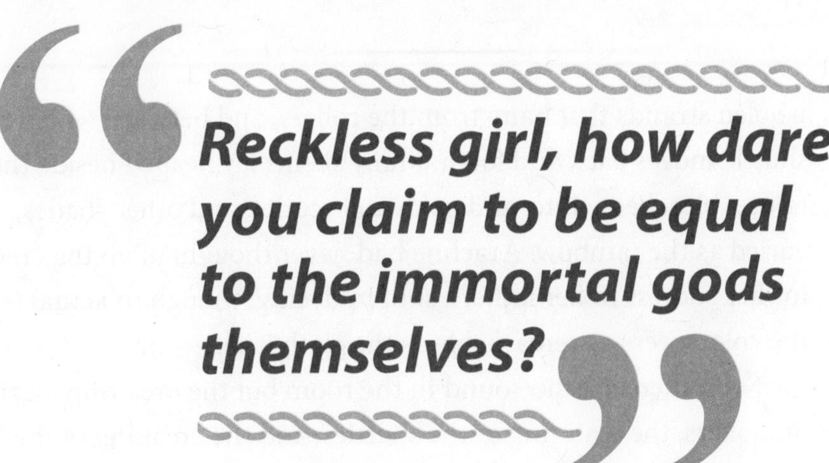

more beautiful embroidery than mine? If Athene herself were to come down and compete with me, she could do no better than I."

One day when Arachne turned round with such words, an old woman answered her, a grey old woman, bent and very poor, who stood leaning on a staff and peering at Arachne amid the crowd of onlookers. "Reckless girl," she said, "how dare you claim to be equal to the immortal gods themselves? I am an old woman and have seen much. Take my advice and ask pardon of Athene for your words. Rest content with your fame of being the best spinner and weaver that mortal eyes have ever beheld."

"Stupid old woman," said Arachne indignantly, "who gave you a right to speak in this way to me? It is easy to see that you were never good for anything in your day, or you would not come here in poverty and rags to gaze at my skill. If Athene resents my words, let her answer them herself. I have challenged her to a contest, but she, of course, will not come. It is easy for the gods to avoid matching their skill with that of men."

At these words the old woman threw down her staff and stood erect. The wondering onlookers saw her grow tall and fair and stand clad in long robes of dazzling white. They were terribly afraid as they realized that they stood in the presence of Athene. Arachne herself flushed red for a moment, for she had never really believed that the goddess would hear her. Before the group that was gathered there she would not give in; so pressing her pale lips together in **obstinacy** and pride, she led the goddess to one of the great looms and set herself before the other. Without a word both began to thread the long

obstinacy:

woolen strands that hang from the rollers, and between which the shuttle moves back and forth. Many skeins lay heaped beside them to use, bleached white, and gold, and scarlet, and other shades, varied as the rainbow. Arachne had never thought of giving credit for her success to her father's skill in dyeing, though in actual truth the colors were as remarkable as the cloth itself.

Soon there was no sound in the room but the breathing of the onlookers, the whirring of the shuttles, and the creaking of the wooden frames as each pressed the thread up into place or tightened the pegs by which the whole was held straight. The excited crowd in the doorway began to see that the skill of both in truth was very nearly equal, but that, however the cloth might turn out, the goddess was the quicker of the two. A pattern of many pictures was growing on her loom. There was a border of twined branches of the olive, Athene's favorite tree, while in the middle, figures began to appear. As they looked at the glowing colors, the spectators realized that Athene was weaving into her pattern a last warning to Arachne. The central figure was the goddess herself competing with Poseidon for possession of the city of Athens; but in the four corners were mortals who had tried to **strive** with gods and pictures of the awful fate that had overtaken them. The goddess ended a little before Arachne and stood back from her marvelous work to see what the maiden was doing.

strive:

4. REREAD Reread lines 38–45. What does the old woman's advice suggest about the theme, or central idea, of the myth?

5. READ As you read lines 68–112, continue to cite textual evidence.

- Underline the warning that Athene weaves into her cloth for Arachne.
- Circle the insult Arachne weaves into her cloth for Athene.
- In the margin, explain what happens to Arachne at the end of the myth.

An ancient Greek statue of Athene

Never before had Arachne been matched against anyone whose skill was equal, or even nearly equal to her own. As she stole glances from time to time at Athene and saw the goddess working swiftly, calmly, and always a little faster than herself, she became angry instead of frightened, and an evil thought came into her head. Thus as Athene stepped back a pace to watch Arachne finishing her work, she saw that the maiden had taken for her design a pattern of scenes which showed evil or unworthy actions of the gods, how they had deceived fair maidens, resorted to trickery, and appeared on earth from time to time in the form of poor and humble people. When the goddess saw this insult glowing in bright colors on Arachne's loom, she did not wait while the cloth was judged, but stepped forward, her grey eyes blazing with anger, and tore Arachne's work across. Then she struck Arachne across the face. Arachne stood there a moment, struggling with anger, fear, and pride. "I will not live under this insult," she cried, and seizing a rope from the wall, she made a noose and would have hanged herself.

descendants:

The goddess touched the rope and touched the maiden. “Live on, wicked girl,” she said. “Live on and spin, both you and your **descendants.** When men look at you they may remember that it is not wise to strive with Athene.” At that the body of Arachne shriveled up, and her legs grew tiny, spindly, and distorted. There before the eyes of the spectators hung a little dusty brown spider on a slender thread.

All spiders descend from Arachne, and as the Greeks watched them spinning their thread wonderfully fine, they remembered the contest with Athene and thought that it was not right for even the best of men to claim equality with the gods.

6. REREAD AND DISCUSS With a small group, discuss what Arachne does to so enrage Athene and whether or not her punishment is justified. Cite text evidence in your discussion.

SHORT RESPONSE

Cite Text Evidence What lessons about human behavior does this myth teach? Review your reading notes, and be sure to **cite text evidence** from the myth in your response.

COLLECTION **2**

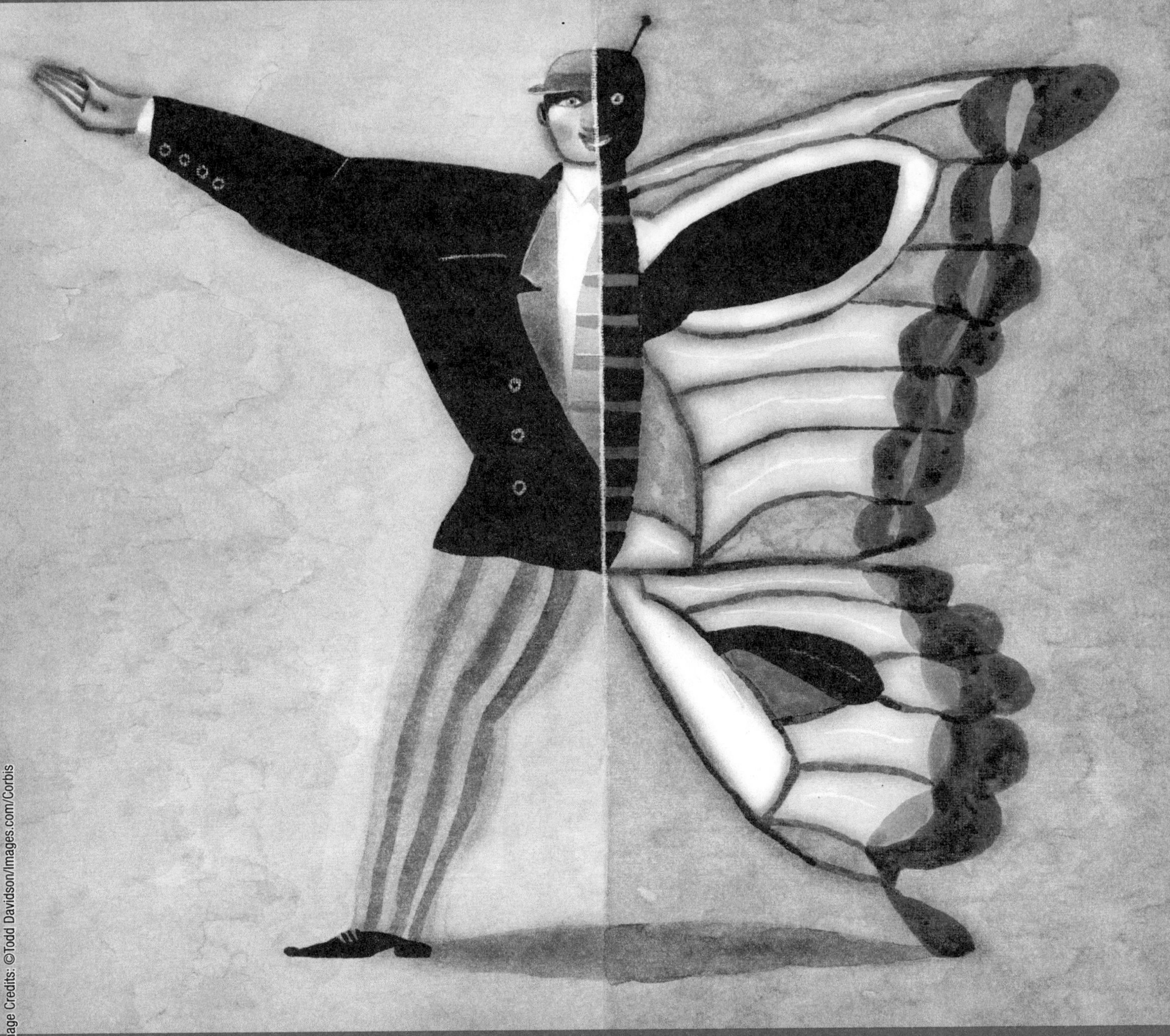

Perception and Reality

COLLECTION **2**

Perception and Reality

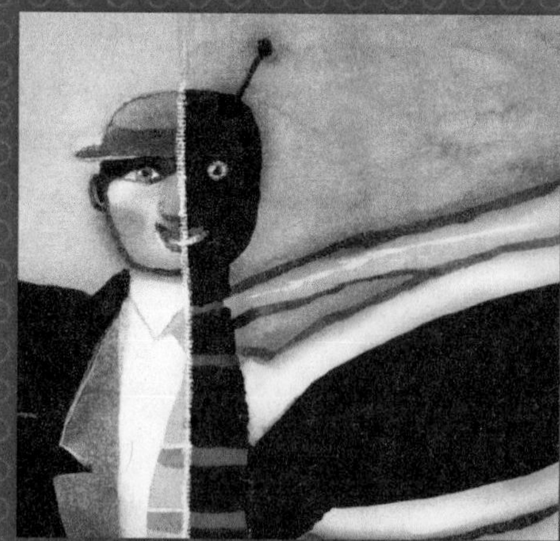

"*Now* I do not know whether it was then I dreamt I was a butterfly, or whether I am now a butterfly, dreaming I am a man."

—Chuang Tzu

Background *Born in 1974,* **David Yoo** *has often felt like an outsider. While attending an international school in Korea, he was the only Korean American student among German and Saudi Arabian classmates. When his family moved to Connecticut, he again encountered few Asian peers. He published his first book,* Girls for Breakfast, *when he was twenty-nine. The book is a humorous account of a Korean-American teenage hero's efforts to fit in at a suburban American high school.*

Heartbeat

Short Story by David Yoo

CLOSE READ Notes

1. **READ ▶** As you read lines 1–36, begin to collect and cite text evidence.
   - Underline adjectives that describe Heartbeat.
   - In the margin, summarize how Heartbeat tries to gain weight.
   - Circle text that reveals how Heartbeat feels when he tries to gain weight.

My nickname's "Heartbeat," because my friends swear that you can actually see the pulse on my bare chest. I've always been skinny. Everyone assumes I'm a weakling because I'm so thin (I prefer "lean and mean" or "wiry"), despite being a three-sport athlete. I decided to do something about it this fall when Sarah, the girl I have a crush on, said, "Oh my gosh . . . you are so skinny." She was visibly repulsed by my sunken chest as I stepped off the soccer bus after practice. I silently vowed to do everything within my power to become the "after" picture. I was sixteen years old, but looked like I was eleven.

For the rest of fall, I did countless push-ups and curled free weights until I couldn't bend my arms. I got ridiculously strong and defined, but I wasn't gaining weight. I wanted to be *thicker.* I didn't care about getting stronger if nobody could tell. I did research, and started lifting heavier weights at lower reps and supplemented my meals with weight-gainer shakes, egg whites, boiled yams, and tubs of

cottage cheese. I forced myself to swallow the daily caloric intake equivalent of three overweight men and still wasn't able to increase my mass. (I have a ridiculously fast metabolism.) Over Christmas break I cut out all useless movement, like Ping-Pong and staircases, because I'm like a sieve—the 83 calories in a mini-Snickers bar is **moot** because I waste 90 chewing it.

moot:

I returned to school in January depressed, because I was still Heartbeat in everyone's eyes. I constantly weighed myself. At least once an hour, no matter where I was, I'd find a bathroom so I could take off my shirt and flex in the mirror for a couple of minutes. I was so frustrated that nothing was working—but the frustration didn't last. I was sitting in study hall two weeks ago when Sarah said the magic words: "Have you been working out, Dave? You look bigger." I couldn't tell if she was being **sarcastic**. I went home and inspected myself in the mirror. I did look bigger!

sarcastic:

But then I realized the reason: I'd accidentally worn *two* T-shirts under my rugby shirt that day. It was just an illusion. I was **futilely** stuffing my face and religiously pumping iron and failing to alter my appearance, and now I'd stumbled on the simplest solution to looking bigger. I felt like I was reborn.

futile:

I went to school the next day wearing two T-shirts under my turtleneck. I felt solid. By the end of last week, I was wearing three

2. REREAD Reread lines 23–31. Circle the narrator's real name. How does he think his classmates perceive him? Support your answer with explicit textual evidence.

____

____

____

3. READ As you read lines 37–75, continue to cite textual evidence.

- Underline the number of T-shirts Heartbeat wears.
- Circle Heartbeat's interpretation of the way his classmates feel when they see him wearing extra layers.

T-shirts under my rugby shirt. This Monday I tucked four T-shirts under my plaid button-down. It gave me traps that didn't exist. My Q-tip-sized shoulders transformed into NBA-grapefruit deltoids.[1] I could tell my classmates subtly regarded me differently. It was respect. Sarah gave me a look I'd never seen before, as if she felt . . . *safer* around me. I was walking down the hallway at the end of the day and must have twisted awkwardly because suddenly my zipper literally exploded, and all my T-shirts spilled out of my pants. Luckily, the hallway was empty and I was wearing a belt.

I realized I had artificially outgrown my clothes. My button-downs were so tight that a few seconds after jamming the extra layers into my pants, the pressure would suddenly bunch the cloth up in random places so it looked like I had a goiter[2] on my shoulder or something. I complained to my parents over dinner last night. "I don't fit into anything anymore," I said. "It reflects poorly on you guys. You could get arrested."

"What are you talking about? You look the same as always. You're still my little boy," my dad replied, putting me in a headlock and giving me a noogie. I glared at him.

"I need a new ski jacket," I said. It was true. I could barely clap my hands with all the layers I was wearing. I was getting out of control at this point. The four T-shirts under my wool sweater were smushing my lungs together like a male girdle. It was a small price to pay; nobody called me Heartbeat anymore, I reminded myself.

After dinner I went to a party. Even though it was winter, I opted to hang out on the back porch as much as possible because it was so

---

[1] **traps...deltoids:** traps (short for trapezius) are large, flat upper-back muscles; deltoids are triangular muscles that connect the top of the shoulder to the arm.

[2] **goiter:** swollen thyroid gland often visible at the bottom of the neck.

hot inside. Being indoors was like a sauna, but Sarah was in the basement so I headed that way. We were talking and she noticed that I was dripping with perspiration. "You're trembling," she said, touching my shoulder. She thought I was nervous talking to her and probably thought it was cute, but in reality I was on the verge of passing out because I was wearing four tight T-shirts and two long-sleeves under my wool sweater, not to mention the sweatpants tucked into my tube socks to add heft to my (formerly chicken-legs) quads. She squeezed my biceps.[3]

"Jeez, Dave, how many layers are you wearing?"

I couldn't even feel her squeezing them.

"I have to go," I said, excusing myself to another corner of the basement. Everyone was smushed together. It was so hot everyone except me was hanging out in T-shirts and tank tops. I was sopping and delirious and felt **claustrophobic**. My chest was cold because I had four drenched T-shirts underneath my sweater. It looked like I was breaking out with Ebola[4] or something. When I coughed people turned away from me in fear. *Abandon ship, abandon ship!* I had no choice but to take some layers off. I lurched to the bathroom. My arms were ponderously heavy as I pulled off the sweater. Just lifting my arms exhausted me, and I had to stop midway and take a rest by sitting on the edge of the tub, gasping. I slowly peeled off the layers, one at a time. I took off my pants and peeled off my sweatpants, too, down to my undies. I dried myself off with a wash cloth. My red T-shirt had bled onto the three white Ts because of the sweat, so they now were faded pink tie-dyes. I hoisted the bundle of clothes and was

claustrophobic:

[3] **quads...biceps:** quads (short for quadriceps) are long muscles in the front of the thigh; biceps are the large muscles in the front of the upper arm.

[4] **Ebola:** deadly virus that causes high fever and bleeding.

4. **◀ REREAD AND DISCUSS** Reread lines 37–44. Dave says, "my classmates subtly regarded me differently. It was with respect." With a small group, discuss whether Dave's assessment of his classmates' response is reality-based or a product of his imagination.

5. **READ ▶** As you read lines 76–113, continue to cite textual evidence.

- Underline adjectives Heartbeat uses to describe himself.
- In the margin, summarize how Heartbeat feels when he sheds his layers at the party.

"I was sopping and delirious and felt claustrophobic."

shocked at the weight. I jammed them into the closet. I'd retrieve them later, before I left. I put my sweater back on without anything underneath. After two weeks of constricting my air supply and range of motion by wearing upwards of six layers, I was amazed at how much freedom I had with my arms. I felt like dancing for the first time in my life. I suddenly realized what I really looked like at this party: a padded, miserable, and frustrated puffball, burning up in all my layers. All this because I hated my nickname?

I got home and realized I'd left my bundle of wet clothes back at the party. I took this as a sign. My days of wearing extra layers was officially over. Had Sarah fallen for the padded me, she'd be falling for someone else. Besides, winter wasn't going to last forever, and I couldn't just revert back to wearing just one set of clothes like a normal human being come spring. The change in my outward appearance would be the equivalent of a sheared sheep. From now on, I was going to just be me.

That was last night. *I'm not disgustingly thin*, I constantly remind myself. I am wiry. I'm lean and mean.

Outside it's snowing again. There's a party tonight, and my friends are on their way to pick me up. I don't know what to wear, so I lay out four different outfits on the floor as if they're chalk outlines of people. A car horn honks ten minutes later and I still haven't decided on an outfit. Maybe I'll just wear all of them.

6. REREAD As you reread lines 76–113, make notes in the margin about why Heartbeat decides he is done wearing extra layers. Then reread the story's final line. Do you think Heartbeat's essential personality has changed? Support your answer with explicit textual evidence.

SHORT RESPONSE

Cite Text Evidence Write a brief summary of the plot of "Heartbeat." Review your reading notes, and use your own words to answer *who? when and where?* and *what happens?* **Cite text evidence** to support your response.

Background *Adrian Owen is a groundbreaking British scientist whose research has been reported in documentaries, on radio and television shows, and in newspapers and magazines. This article presents the remarkable discoveries Owen brought to light as he studied the brain activity of a special group of people.*

Saving the Lost

Science Article by Reynaldo Vasquez

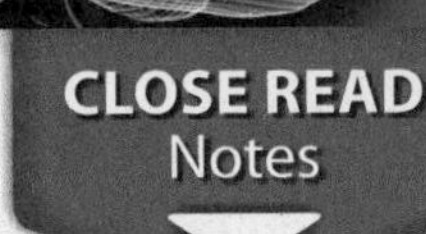

1. **READ ▶** As you read lines 1–14, begin to collect and cite text evidence.
   - Circle the question at the beginning of the article.
   - Underline the central idea in the first paragraph, and paraphrase the idea in the margin.
   - Underline the central idea in the second paragraph, and restate it in the margin.

How can we understand what a person who cannot respond is thinking or feeling? People in a *vegetative state* are those who have come out of a coma and appear to be awake with open eyes and sleep patterns. However, they do not show any awareness of who they are or where they are. They cannot speak and do not respond to sounds, hunger, or pain. The actual condition of patients in a vegetative state mostly remained a secret until Adrian Owen made some startling discoveries.

In the late 1990s, British scientist Owen realized that the technology of *neuroimaging*—producing images of brain activity without surgery—supported what scientists already knew. Different parts of the brain process different kinds of thoughts. Owen's concern was that neuroimaging was breaking no new ground. He wanted to find a real use for it.

> STRANGE AS IT SOUNDS, SCIENTISTS KNOW THE PART OF THE BRAIN THAT SHOWS ACTIVITY IN HEALTHY PEOPLE WHEN THEY IMAGINE PLAYING TENNIS. IT IS ALWAYS THE SAME.

rehabilitation:

In 1997, Owen and his team began testing a patient who was in a vegetative state. They scanned her brain as they showed her familiar faces, and "it lit up like a Christmas tree." Based on these results, the patient was given intense **rehabilitation**—whereas in many cases, people in a vegetative state are simply kept alive. She has since sent a letter to thank Owen, realizing that without the brain scan, she too would have been written off.

Owen continued his research, and in 2006 he made another breakthrough. He took brain scans of a woman patient as he asked her to imagine playing tennis. Strange as it sounds, scientists know the part of the brain that shows activity in healthy people when they imagine playing tennis. It is always the same. It was the same in his patient, too. He asked his patient to imagine walking through her home. Her brain showed activity in the exact same spot as healthy

2. **◀ REREAD** Reread lines 9–14. Summarize Adrian Owen's challenge and the medical mystery he hoped to solve. Support your answer with explicit textual evidence.

3. **READ ▶** As you read lines 15–33, continue to cite textual evidence.
   - Circle the time-order words or phrases that signal the sequence of events.
   - In the margin, explain the advantage of using chronological order to organize the text.

people would if they thought of walking through the rooms of their homes. Owen believed that this showed that the patient was conscious. Some researchers agreed with Owen, while others disagreed. They believed that the response was an involuntary reaction to the final words that Owen said to the patient.

Owen did not give up. With a team from Belgium, he tested 54 other patients. Of these, five responded in the same way as his previous patient. Then they reached a huge breakthrough studying "patient 23." He had been in a vegetative state for five years following a car accident. The scientists discovered that patient 23 was able to give "yes" and "no" answers by changing his brain activity. They asked him questions with answers that the **technicians** couldn't know, and that weren't given away by any clues.

technician:

"Is your father's name Thomas?"

"No."

"Is your father's name Alexander?"

"Yes."

"Do you have any brothers?"

"Yes."

"Do you have any sisters?"

"No."

When Owen published his discovery in 2010, there was an immediate response from the media and the scientific community. A Canadian university offered a huge amount of funding for Owen to continue his research there.

4. **◀ REREAD** Reread lines 22–33. Summarize the events that took place in 2006. Support your answer with explicit textual evidence.

5. **READ ▶** Read lines 34–60. Underline each central idea, and in the margin, write at least one supporting detail.

There are neuroscientists who do not agree with Owen's conclusions and who argue about the point at which consciousness can be said to exist. Owen is not interested in such details. In the United States, there are tens of thousands of people in vegetative states. Owen thinks that perhaps one-fifth of these people could be able to communicate. He would like to see that possibility become a reality.

6. **REREAD AND DISCUSS** Reread lines 34–49. With a small group, discuss the reasons the author includes dialogue in this passage.

SHORT RESPONSE

Cite Text Evidence Using specific details from the text, write a short summary of Owen's work and its possible consequences. **Cite text evidence** to support your response.

Background **Charles Dickens's** *novel* A Christmas Carol *tells the story of Ebenezer Scrooge, a miserly old man who is transformed by extraordinary encounters with his own past, present, and future. Dickens's tale has been retold many times. It was adapted into a play by American playwright* **Israel Horovitz** *and retold as a graphic story by* **Marvel Comics.** *You will read three versions of a scene from* A Christmas Carol. *In the scene that follows, Scrooge is being led to a graveyard by the Ghost of Christmas Yet to Come.*

COMPARING VERSIONS OF

A Christmas Carol

1. **READ ▶** As you read lines 1–30, begin to cite text evidence.
   - Underline details that describe the setting.
   - Circle the questions Scrooge asks the spirit.
   - In the margin, summarize what happens in lines 28–30.

from A Christmas Carol
Novel by Charles Dickens

"Specter," said Scrooge, "something informs me that our parting moment is at hand. I know it, but I know not how. Tell me what man that was, with the covered face, whom we saw lying dead?"

The Ghost of Christmas Yet to Come conveyed him to a **dismal**, wretched, ruinous churchyard.

dismal:

The spirit stood among the graves, and pointed down to one.

"Before I draw nearer to that stone to which you point, answer me one question. Are these the shadows of the things that will be, or are they shadows of the things that may be only?"

Still the ghost pointed downward to the grave by which it stood.

"Men's courses will foreshadow certain ends, to which, if persevered in, they must lead. But if the courses be departed from, the ends will change. Say it is thus with what you show me!"

The spirit was immovable as ever.

Scrooge crept toward it, trembling as he went; and following the finger, read upon the stone of the neglected grave his own name—EBENEZER SCROOGE.

"Am I that man who lay upon the bed? No, Spirit! Oh no, no! Spirit! hear me! I am not the man I was. I will not be the man I must have been but for this intercourse. Why show me this, if I am past all hope? Assure me that I yet may change these shadows you have shown me, by an **altered** life."

altered:

For the first time the kind hand faltered.

"I will honor Christmas in my heart, and try to keep it all the year. I will live in the Past, the Present, and the Future. The spirits of all three shall strive within me. I will not shut out the lessons that they teach. Oh, tell me I may sponge away the writing on this stone!"

Holding up his hands in one last prayer to have his fate reversed, he saw an alteration in the phantom's hood and dress. It shrunk, collapsed, and dwindled down into a bedpost.

2. **◀ REREAD** Reread lines 1–30. What effect do Scrooge's repeated questions achieve?

SHORT RESPONSE

Cite Text Evidence Scrooge is the only character who speaks in the scene. Which details show that the spirit is affected by what Scrooge says? **Cite text evidence** in your response.

CLOSE READ Notes

3. READ ▶ As you read lines 1–28, continue to cite textual evidence.

- Underline every sentence that mentions Future's hand.
- Circle the special effects in the stage directions.
- In the margin, note an element in this drama that is not in the original story.

from A Christmas Carol: Scrooge and Marley

Drama by Israel Horovitz

Scrooge. Specter, something informs me that our parting moment is at hand. I know it, but I know not how I know it.

[FUTURE *points to the other side of the stage. Lights out on* CRATCHITS.[1] FUTURE *moves slowing, gliding.* SCROOGE *follows.* FUTURE *points opposite.* FUTURE *leads* SCROOGE *to a wall and a tombstone. He points to the stone.*]

Am *I* that man those ghoulish parasites[2] so gloated over? (*Pauses*) Before I draw nearer to that stone to which you point, answer me one question. Are these the shadows of things that will be, or the shadows of things that MAY be, only?

[FUTURE *points to the gravestone.* MARLEY[3] *appears in light well* UPSTAGE. *He points to grave as well. Gravestone turns front and grows to ten feet high. Words upon it*: EBENEZER SCROOGE. *Much smoke billows now from the grave. Choral music here.* SCROOGE *stands looking up at gravestone.* FUTURE *does not at all reply in mortals' words, but points once more to the gravestone. The stone undulates and glows. Music plays, beckoning* SCROOGE. SCROOGE, *reeling in terror*]

---

[1] **Crachits:** The family of Bob Crachit, Scrooge's clerk. He is mistreated and underpaid by Scrooge.

[2] **ghoulish parasites:** people who stole Scrooge's possessions and divided them up after he died.

[3] **Marley:** Scrooge's business partner, deceased at the time of the events in the drama. He appears to Scrooge as a ghost.

"Spirit! Hear me! I am not the man I was."

Oh, no, Spirit! Oh, no, no!

[FUTURE's *finger still pointing*]

Spirit! Hear me! I am not the man I was. I will not be the man I would have been but for this intercourse. Why show me this, if I am past all hope?

[FUTURE *considers* SCROOGE's *logic. His hand wavers.*]

Oh, Good Spirit, I see by your wavering hand that your good nature intercedes for me and pities me. Assure me that I yet may change these shadows that you have shown me by an altered life!

[FUTURE's *hand trembles; pointing has stopped.*]

I will honor Christmas in my heart and try to keep it all the year. I will live in the Past, the Present, and the Future. The Spirits of all Three shall strive within me. I will not shut out the lessons that they teach. Oh, tell me that I may sponge away the writing that is upon this stone!

[SCROOGE *makes a desperate stab at grabbing* FUTURE's *hand. He holds it firm for a moment, but* FUTURE, *stronger than* SCROOGE, *pulls away.* SCROOGE *is on his knees, praying.*]

Spirit, dear Spirit, I am praying before you. Give me a sign that all is possible. Give me a sign that all hope for me is not lost. Oh, Spirit, kind Spirit, I beseech thee: give me a sign . . .

4. **REREAD AND DISCUSS** Reread lines 1–28. In a small group, discuss why Future stops pointing.

5. **READ** As you read lines 29–44, continue to cite textual evidence.

- Underline the promise that Scrooge makes.
- Circle the stage directions.
- Note in the margin what Scrooge wants in lines 37–39.

[FUTURE *deliquesces,*[4] *slowly, gently. The* PHANTOM's *hood and robe drop gracefully to the ground in a small heap. Music in. There is nothing in them. They are mortal cloth. The* SPIRIT *is elsewhere.* SCROOGE *has his sign.* SCROOGE *is alone. Tableau. The lights fade to black.*]

[4] **deliquesces:** melts away; dissolves.

6. **◀ REREAD** Reread lines 34–36. What do the stage directions reveal about Scrooge's emotions? Cite textual evidence in your answer.

SHORT RESPONSE

Cite Text Evidence How is this experience of reading a dramatization of *A Christmas Carol* different from reading the original story? Analyze elements such as stage directions and dialogue. Use your reading notes and be sure to **cite text evidence** in your response.

7. READ ▶ As you read this page, begin to collect and cite text evidence.

- Circle examples of Scrooge's facial expressions.
- Circle text that shows Scrooge trying to convince or influence the spirit.
- In the margin, explain what Scrooge wants to know from the spirit.

from A Christmas Carol

Graphic Story by Marvel Comics

8. ◀ REREAD What do Scrooge's facial expressions tell you about his feelings about the Ghost of Christmas Future?

9. **READ ▶** As you read this page, continue to cite textual evidence.

- Circle what Scrooge sees on the tombstone.
- Circle text that reveals that Scrooge wants to change.
- In the margin, explain what happens to the Ghost of Christmas Future.

CLOSE READ
Notes

10. REREAD AND DISCUSS In a small group, discuss which was most effective in conveying the change in Scrooge: the text or the illustrations. Cite text evidence in your discussion.

SHORT RESPONSE

Cite Text Evidence Is the change in Scrooge's character most believable in the novel, the drama, or the graphic story? **Cite text evidence** in your response.

COLLECTION 3

Nature at Work

COLLECTION **3**

Nature at Work

"Those who dwell . . . among the beauties and mysteries of the earth are never alone or weary of life."

—Rachel Carson

Background **Helen Thayer** *is a decorated explorer and adventurer. Her achievements include being the first woman to walk across the Sahara Desert, kayaking 1,200 miles across two rivers in the Amazon, and walking 1,600 miles across the Gobi Desert in Asia. In 1988, at the age of 50, she became the first woman to walk and ski to the North Pole without a snowmobile or dogsled. She wrote about her adventure in* Polar Dream.

from Polar Dream

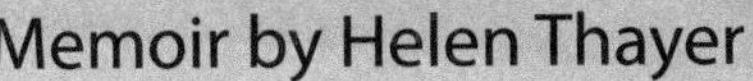

Memoir by Helen Thayer

1. READ ▷ As you read lines 1–64, begin to collect and cite evidence.

- Circle the metaphor in the second sentence, and explain the meaning of it in the margin.
- Underline items Thayer wears to stay warm.
- Write in the margin why it's important for Thayer to stay hydrated.

I woke at 5:30 A.M. after a restless night's sleep. My hands were blistered clubs and hurt every time I touched something. Overnight enormous blood blisters had formed to reach all the way down to the second joint of each finger except my left little finger, which had somehow escaped freezing. I knew I had to keep the blisters intact so that my hands wouldn't become raw and bleeding. It would be better to use my heavy mitts as much as possible even though they were clumsy. I thought back to the previous morning, remembering the crazy repacking of my sled with gear ending up in all the wrong places as I just stood there not wanting to offend anyone. I decided what is done is done. One learns one's lessons the hard way sometimes and, besides, if that was to be the only problem of the whole expedition, then I would consider myself lucky.

Reaching over I painfully and slowly unzipped the tent door to inspect the new day. Just like yesterday. The wind had dropped. I looked out at cold, clear skies and a light northerly wind. Another

CLOSE READ
Notes

beautiful Arctic day. Charlie was up and looking at his empty bowl. I crawled out of my sleeping bag, creating a minor snowstorm as I brushed against the frost-covered tent roof while I pulled on my jacket. I'm normally a morning person but there was something about the intense cold, the tent frost down my neck, and my sore hands that made that morning most unappealing. But it was time to greet Charlie and start the day.

sly:

Stepping out of the tent, still in my insulated blue camp booties, I checked the thermometer, minus 41 degrees. I looked around for bears or tracks and saw none, but I was surprised to notice that the shore ice with its jagged blocks and pinnacles ended only one hundred feet from my tent. In the settling light of last evening it had looked as if I was at least four hundred yards from the closest rough shore ice. It was my first lesson in the **sly** nature of the changing Arctic light and the way it affected depth perception.

Charlie was bouncing up and down at the end of his chain looking well rested. I hugged him good morning as his soft tongue wiped across my face. I poured what looked like a pound of dog food into his bowl, which he attacked with gusto.

Now for my stove. I simply had to light it that morning. I needed water for the next leg of my journey and a hot breakfast would get my day started off right. I carefully put a pair of woollen gloves over my liners and with clenched teeth I forced my cruelly protesting fingers to push the stove tube into the gasket at the top of the fuel bottle. Success. I lit it, put snow and ice into my two-quart pan, and soon had warm water. To conserve fuel, I heated water only to a temperature at which I could still put my finger into it.

It was only six o'clock, so I decided to have a leisurely breakfast of a bowl of granola, milk powder, coconut flakes, raisins, and butter mixed with warm water. I sat on my sled to enjoy the full effect of my first breakfast of the expedition only to find that after the third spoonful it was frozen. So much for leisurely breakfasts! I added more warm water and ate the rest as fast as possible. Then I melted enough ice to fill two vacuum bottles with water and a carbohydrate powder.

The dry Arctic air holds little moisture, causing quick dehydration of the body, which, in turn, causes early fatigue and reduces the body's ability to keep warm, so fluid would be just as important as food to keep my energy reserves up. I put my day's supply of crackers, cashews, walnuts, and peanut butter cups in my day food bag along with the two vacuum bottles and slipped everything down into the front of the sled bag. Then, remembering Charlie's appetite for crackers, I added a few more.

Last to be packed was the tent. I was completely **engrossed** in finding a way to twist the tent ice screws out of the ice so that my hands wouldn't scream in protest when suddenly I heard a deep, long growl coming from the depths of Charlie's throat. In a flash I looked at him and then in the direction in which he was staring. I knew what I would see even before I looked. A polar bear!

engrossed:

It was a female followed by two cubs coming from Bathurst Island,[1] slowly, purposefully, plodding through the rough shore ice toward me. They were two hundred yards away. With a pounding heart I grabbed my loaded rifle and flare gun and carefully walked sideways a few steps to Charlie, who was snarling with a savagery that caught my breath. Without taking my eyes off the bear, I unclipped Charlie from his ice anchor and, again walking sideways, I led him to the sled where I clipped his chain to a tie-down rope. The bear, now only 150 yards away, wasn't stopping. Her cubs had dropped back but she came on with a steady measured stride while I frantically tried to remember all the Inuit[2] had told me. Keep eye contact, move sideways

[1] **Bathurst Island:** an uninhabited island that is part of the Canadian Arctic Archipelago.

[2] **Inuit:** a group of people belonging to the Eskimo family who live throughout the Canadian Artic.

2. **REREAD AND DISCUSS** Reread lines 59–64. In a small group, discuss whether Thayer seems prepared for the situation that occurs.

3. **READ** As you read lines 65–103, continue to cite textual evidence.
   - Underline what Thayer was told to do if a polar bear approached her.
   - Circle figurative language that describes how Thayer feels during the encounter with the polar bear.
   - In the margin, explain what this figurative language conveys about Thayer.

> *Don't wound a bear, you'll make it even more dangerous. . . .*

or slightly forward, never backward, stay calm, don't show fear, stand beside a tent, sled, or other large object to make my five feet three inches appear as large as possible. Don't shoot unless forced to. Don't wound a bear, you'll make it even more dangerous, and never run. Repeating to myself, "Stay calm, stay calm," I fired a warning shot to the bear's left. The loud explosion of the .338 had no effect. On she came. I fired a flare, landing it a little to her right. Her head moved slightly in its direction but she didn't stop. I fired another flare, this time dropping it right in front of her. She stopped, looked at the flare burning a bright red on the white ice, then looked at me. She was only one hundred feet away now.

By this time my nerves were as tight as violin strings and my heart could have been heard at base camp. The bear began to step around the flare, and I dropped another flare two feet in front of her. Again she stopped, looked at the flare and at me. Then she fixed her tiny black eyes on Charlie, who was straining at the end of his chain, snapping and snarling trying to reach her. She looked back at her cubs. I could sense her concern about Charlie's snarling, **rabid** act and her cubs. She waited for her cubs to catch up, then moved to my left in a half circle. In spite of my sore fingers I fired two more flares in quick succession, trying to draw a line between her and me. She stopped, then moved back toward my right. I fired two more flares and again she stopped. She seemed to want to cross the line of flares but was unsure of the result and of Charlie, so she elected to stay back.

rabid:

She kept moving right in a half circle, still one hundred feet away. Finally, with a last long look she plodded north with her two new cubs trotting behind her, their snow-white coats contrasting with their mother's creamy, pale yellow color.

The whole episode lasted fifteen minutes but seemed years long. I was a nervous wreck. My hands were shaking as I stood still holding my rifle and flare gun, watching the trio slowly move north. But in spite of the mind-numbing fear that still gripped me, I could feel deep down inside a real satisfaction. I now knew that I could stand up to a bear in the wild, stay calm enough to function and still remember the words of wisdom from the Inuit. With Charlie's help I had passed my first test. The bear had been completely silent as it had approached and moved around me on paws thickly padded with fur on the undersides. I was thankful for Charlie's warning. Now he had stopped growling and snarling but still stood rigid, watching the bears as they zigzagged in and out of the rough ice hunting for the seals that lived in the cold waters beneath the ice. He seemed to hardly notice the giant hug I gave him. He was still on guard.

The bears were only about four hundred yards away but I decided to continue packing my tent and move around to stay warm, still keeping a wary eye on the bears. I was getting cold. My fear and flowing adrenaline had kept me warm but I was beginning to shiver

4. **REREAD** Reread lines 65–86. The writer could have used many short sentences to retell the advice she received. What is the effect of retelling all the advice she received in three sentences?

5. **READ** As you read lines 104–129, continue to cite textual evidence.

- Underline the emotions Thayer feels after the polar bear leaves.
- Make notes in the margin about why Thayer is grateful to Charlie.
- Circle words that describe the polar bear.

now. I finished packing and stood around until ten o'clock, keeping warm, until I was sure the bears had disappeared and weren't circling back to me. If I stayed out from the coast, keeping away from the rough ice, I hoped to make up the time I had lost. But as I started out I still thought about the bears. Even as frightened as I had been, it was a thrill to see a bear and her cubs in their natural environment. She was unafraid of me, powerful and dangerous, yet graceful. And she was a tender, attentive mother caring for her cubs.

6. REREAD Reread lines 104–129. How does the author's specific word choice convey the importance of this experience to her? Support your answer with explicit textual evidence.

SHORT RESPONSE

Cite Text Evidence Analyze the way Thayer uses a particular style to convey the meaning of events in the text. Include examples of words and phrases as they are used in the text, such as figurative language and specific word choice. Be sure to review your reading notes and **cite text evidence** in your response.

Background *Canyonlands National Park in southeast Utah contains countless canyons, mesas, buttes, and other odd rock formations created by the Colorado and Green rivers. The environmental essayist Edward Abbey has described the park as "the most weird, wonderful, magical place on earth—there is nothing else like it anywhere." In this essay, you will discover the reason why some elite adventurers come to explore the park.*

The Hidden Southwest: The Arch Hunters

Essay by James Vlahos

CLOSE READ Notes

1. **READ ▶** As you read lines 1–22, begin to collect and cite text evidence.
   - Circle the repeated statement in lines 1–10.
   - In the margin, state in your own words the central (or main) idea the repeated statement expresses.
   - Underline the supporting details in lines 1–22 that develop the central idea.

The rock arch is lost. It's around here somewhere but could be anywhere; we've searched all morning and gotten nowhere. Picking my way through boulders and gnarled junipers, I reach the scalloped rim of a high mesa and peer over the edge. My stomach drops.

This part of Canyonlands National Park is known as the Needles District, a name too tidy to describe the slickrock chaos erupting from the valley below. There are knobs, blobs, towers, and fins, an array containing every shape of sculpted rock save the one we're seeking. The arch is lost.

Two men join me on the overlook. The first wears a plaid Western shirt neatly tucked into blue Levi's. Leathery, all limbs and no body fat, he steps **nimbly** to the precipice. "Did you talk to Alex Ranney?" he is saying.

nimbly:

CLOSE READ
Notes

"I did," replies the second man. Wearing a khaki shirt, shorts, and mirrored sunglasses, he looks like a refugee from a Kalahari game drive.

"Did you get any more clues?" asks Western Shirt.

"Nope, Ranney was elusive," replies Sunglasses.

"Tight-lipped."

"Totally. He said, 'I want you to be able to find it yourself and get the thrill of discovery.'"

The rock formation we seek is a quadruple arch known as Klingon Battle Cruiser. The first recorded sighting wasn't until 1994 by Ranney, a canyoneer from Tucson, Arizona. Not on any map or trail, it has probably been glimpsed by fewer than a dozen people in the history of the park. Tom Budlong (Western Shirt) and Tom Van Bebber (Sunglasses) desperately want to add their names to the list. These guys are no casual tourists. Rather, they are arch hunters.

Few sights are as celebrated in—or as iconic of—the American West as the natural rock arch. Arches have astounded generations of desert wanderers, from Teddy Roosevelt, who camped below Rainbow Bridge in 1913, to Edward Abbey, who memorably **venerated** them in *Desert Solitaire*. America's spans are internationally recognizable wonders on par with Old Faithful and Half Dome, their shapes burned into the collective consciousness by countless photographs and films.

venerate: regard with great respect

Rock shouldn't take flight in the sky; when it does, in scorn of known physical laws, people take notice. Arches National Park, America's best known repository of spans, draws more than 800,000 visitors each year from around the world. Yet despite such obvious attraction, few consider searching outside park boundaries—even

2. **REREAD** Reread lines 1–22. Use the central idea and the supporting details to write a summary of the first two paragraphs.

They were in ah on what they found and are telling every one about it

3. **READ** As you read lines 23–45, continue to cite textual evidence.

- Circle the specific reason the arch hunters are in the park.
- Underline the details that suggest that a rock arch is an extraordinary sight.

though the Colorado Plateau has the highest density of rock arches worldwide. There are at least 2,000 stone spans scattered throughout the Four Corners states.

Budlong and Van Bebber belong to the world's **preeminent**, and perhaps only, arch-hunting club—NABS, the Natural Arch and Bridge Society. Its 110 members scour the globe by plane, boat, 4x4, and foot. They prowl Antarctic islands, Algerian sands, and the canyons of the American Southwest. True explorers, they live for the moment of discovery: rounding a canyon bend to spot a miracle of natural engineering that perhaps nobody else in the world has ever seen.

preeminent:

In the case of Klingon Battle Cruiser, that moment of revelation is proving hard to come by. Van Bebber had invited me along on a week's worth of arch hunting, hoping I might catch the fever. This is not an encouraging start. He examines a map, scratches his chin, and sighs, "It's probably just right below us."

I leave the pair to study their charts and hike several hundred yards along the rim. Looking down at an expanse of tawny rock, I realize I am gazing *through* it—through a yawning window at the tiny green dots of trees in the valley below. Nearby, I see three additional **portals**. "Over here!" I shout.

portals:

I step carefully from the canyon rim onto the top of the arch and feel a swirl of vertigo. After it subsides I take a second step, then a third, following a rock catwalk into blue sky. Reaching the apex I rotate slowly around, a full 360 degrees, the canyon bottom hundreds of feet straight below.

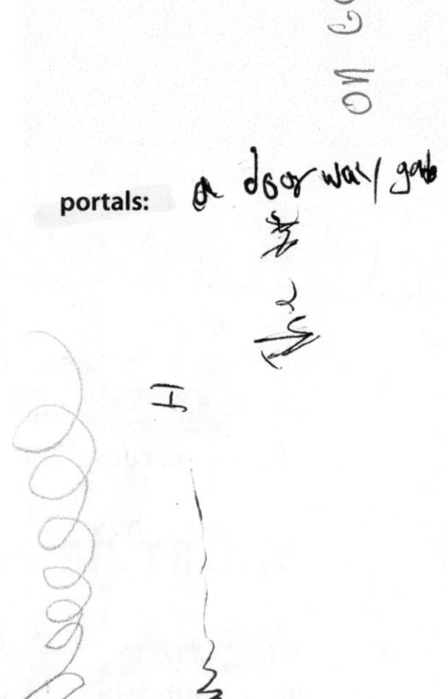

Worldwide, arches number in the tens of thousands, and probably no place is better suited to their formation than the Colorado Plateau. The sandstone is porous and erosive. The geological strata are such that harder layers lie atop weaker ones; the softer rock erodes from

4. **◀ REREAD AND DISCUSS** Reread lines 23–45. With a small group discuss the reasons why adventurers seek out rock arches.

5. **READ ▶** As you read lines 46–88, continue to cite textual evidence.
   - In the margin, paraphrase the reason why the writer says Budlong and Van Bebber are true explorers.
   - Circle the sentences that show that the narrator has found the arch.
   - Underline the sentences in lines 77–88 that reveal an unexpected discovery.

below to leave an arch standing above. And finally, the plateau is in the midst of a rapid geological uplift. Cliff walls push higher while at the same time rivers and meltwater carve deeper and faster. The twin forces produce the critical fins and cracks.

A day after finding Klingon Battle Cruiser, I stand at the base of an **undulating** mass of slickrock, a natural staircase of narrow benches and tilted slopes. With Van Bebber's outstretched palms providing a necessary toehold on blank rock, I scramble up to the first shelf. After walking along it until I find a low-angle passage, I clamber to the next level of the staircase, and the next. A few hundred yards upslope is my goal: the massive triangular portal of Cleft Arch. The only visible route up to the fourth and final bench, however, is too steep. Frustrated, I follow the shelf south and round a corner to make a startling discovery. Tucked under an overhang, invisible until I'm right upon it, is an Anasazi ruin with three well-preserved walls of neatly stacked stone. Arch hunting, I'm learning, often yields much more than the arches themselves.

undulating: having a smoothly rising and falling form or outline

6. REREAD Reread lines 70–75. Write an explanation in the margin of the cause-and-effect connection between events in these lines.

SHORT RESPONSE

Cite Text Evidence What is the central idea of the essay? Consider the important details the writer conveys about rock arches in the text. Review your reading notes, and **cite text evidence** in your response.

The main idea is finding out the form of these rocks. they are different and are hard to find in the world

Background *Nature has been an inspiration to poets and writers for thousands of years. Whether it's the soothing view of a sunset over the ocean or the startling sound of thunder in a rainstorm, nature can excite the senses and the imaginations of all people. The following three poems present different views on three aspects of nature.*

Poems About Nature

Victor Hernández Cruz *was born in Puerto Rico in 1949. When he was five, his family moved to New York City. He began writing at the age of 15. His lively, often humorous poems reflect his bilingual and bicultural heritage. Cruz is the author of numerous poetry collections and the recipient of many awards.*

Leslie Marmon Silko *was born in Albuquerque, New Mexico, in 1948. She grew up on the Laguna Pueblo reservation. Her mixed ancestry (Laguna Pueblo, Mexican, and Caucasian) caused her a lot of pain, as she faced discriminatation from both the Native American and white communities. She would go on to write stories that explore how differences can be reconciled.*

Gwendolyn Brooks *was born in Kansas in 1917, but grew up in Chicago. She published her first poem when she was 14 years old. By the time she was 17, over one hundred of her poems were published in a poetry column in the* Chicago Defender. *She went on to become the first African American author to win the Pulitzer Prize.*

1. READ ▶ As you read "Problems with Hurricanes," collect and cite textual evidence.
   - In the first stanza, underline what the campesino says to worry about.
   - Circle words the campesino uses to assess various ways of dying. In the margin, note the distinction he makes.
   - In the margin, write why the campesino warns of "beautiful sweet things" (lines 34–35).

Problems with Hurricanes

by Victor Hernández Cruz

A campesino[1] looked at the air
And told me:
With hurricanes it's not the wind
or the noise or the water.
I'll tell you he said:
it's the mangoes, avocados
Green plantains and bananas
flying into town like **projectiles**.

projectile:

How would your family
feel if they had to tell
The generations that you
got killed by a flying
Banana.

Death by drowning has honor
If the wind picked you up
and slammed you
Against a mountain boulder
This would not carry shame
But
to suffer a mango smashing
Your skull
or a plantain hitting your
Temple at 70 miles per hour
is the ultimate disgrace.

[1] **campesino** (kăm-pĭ-sē´-nō): a farm worker.

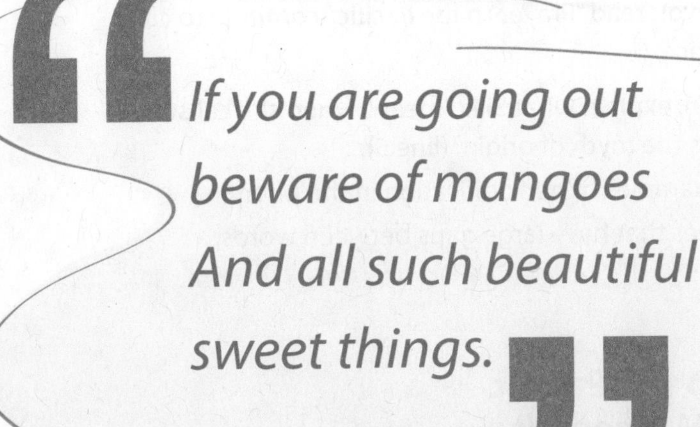

The campesino takes off his hat—
As a sign of respect
toward the fury of the wind
And says:
Don't worry about the noise
Don't worry about the water
Don't worry about the wind—
If you are going out
beware of mangoes
And all such beautiful
sweet things.

2. **REREAD** Reread the poem. What does the speaker suggest about nature in lines 32–35? What broader message about life might he be conveying?

3. READ ▶ As you read "Prayer to the Pacific," continue to cite textual evidence.

- In the margin, explain what Silko means when she calls the ocean "Big as the myth of origin" (line 5).
- Underline examples of personification in the poem.
- Circle the lines that have large gaps between words.

Prayer to the Pacific
by Leslie Marmon Silko

I traveled to the ocean
distant
from my southwest land of sandrock
to the moving blue water
Big as the myth of origin.
Pale
pale water in the yellow-white light of
sun   floating west
to China
where ocean herself was born.
Clouds that blow across the sand are wet.

Squat in the wet sand and speak to the Ocean:
I return to you turquoise the red coral you sent us,
sister spirit of Earth.
Four round stones in my pocket I carry back the ocean
Thirty thousand years ago to suck and to taste.
Indians came riding across the ocean
carried by giant sea turtles.
Waves were high that day
great sea turtles waded   slowly out
from the gray sundown sea.
Grandfather Turtle rolled in the sand   four times
and disappeared
swimming into the sun.

And so from that time
immemorial,
as the old people say,
rain clouds drift from the west
gift from the ocean.
Green leaves in the wind
Wet earth on my feet
swallowing raindrops
clear from China.

immemorial:

4. REREAD Reread the poem and note the lines you circled. What is the effect of separating words within a line? What does it contribute to the meaning of the poem? Support your answer with explicit textual evidence.

5. **READ ▶** As you read "Tornado At Talladega," continue to cite textual evidence.

- Underline examples of personification in the poem.
- Circle examples of repetition.

Tornado at Talladega
by Gwendolyn Brooks

Who is that bird
reporting the storm?—
after What came through
to do some landscaping.

Certain trees
stick across the road.
They are unimportant now.
They cannot sass anymore.
Not a one of these, the bewildered,
can announce anymore "How fine I am!"
Here, roots, **ire**, origins exposed,
across this twig-strewn, leaf-strewn road they lie,
mute, and ashamed, and through.

It happened all of a sudden.

Certain women and men and children
come out to stare.

ire:

6. **◀ REREAD AND DISCUSS** Reread the poem. In a small group, discuss the way personification affects your perception of the trees.

SHORT RESPONSE

Cite Text Evidence How does each poet present nature in these poems? Review your reading notes and **cite text evidence** in your response.

Risk and Exploration

COLLECTION 4

Risk and Exploration

"All adventures, especially into new territory, are scary."

—Sally Ride

ONLINE ESSAY

Is Space Exploration Worth the Cost?

Joan Vernikos

NEWSPAPER ARTICLE

Stinging Tentacles Offer Hint of Oceans' Decline

Elisabeth Rosenthal

Background *Beginning in 1981, NASA launched American astronauts into outer space through the Space Shuttle Program. However, budget cuts forced NASA to discontinue the shuttle program in 2011. For years, scientists and economists have debated whether NASA should carry out human space travel in the future. As Director of NASA's Life Sciences Division,* **Dr. Joan Vernikos** *studied the harmful effects of weightlessness on astronauts.*

Is Space Exploration Worth the Cost?

Online Essay by Joan Vernikos

CLOSE READ Notes

1. READ ▶ As you read lines 1–31, begin to collect and cite evidence.
   - Circle the question at the beginning of the essay.
   - In the margin, explain what Vernikos says about the human spirit in lines 5–7.
   - Then, underline the main idea in each of the next two paragraphs.

Why explore? Asked why he kept trying to climb Everest, English mountaineer George Mallory reputedly replied, "Because it was there." Exploration is intrinsic to our nature. It is the contest between man and nature mixed with the primal desire to conquer. It fuels curiosity, inspiration and creativity. The human spirit seeks to discover the unknown, and in the process explore the physical and psychological potential of human **endurance**.

endurance:

There have always been the few risk-takers who ventured for the rest of us to follow. Because of earlier pioneers, air travel is now commonplace, and space travel for all is just around the corner. Economic and societal benefits are not immediately evident, but they always follow, as does our understanding of human potential to overcome challenges. Fifty years after Sputnik,[1] space remains the next frontier.

[1] **Sputnik:** the world's first artificial satellite was put into orbit around Earth by the Soviet Union on October 4, 1957. Its launch marked the start of the space age.

Without risking human lives, robotic technology such as unmanned missions, probes, observatories, and landers enables space exploration. It lays the groundwork, and does the scouting. But as I heard former astronaut Thomas Jones often say, "only a human can experience what being in space feels like, and only a human can communicate this to others." It is humans who repair the Hubble telescope.[2] It is humans who service the International Space Station (ISS). Mercury astronauts were the first to photograph Earth from space with hand-held cameras. Earth scientists in orbit on the ISS may view aspects of global change that only a trained eye can see. In addition, studying astronauts in the microgravity of space has been the only means of understanding how gravity affects human development and health here on Earth. It is highly probable that, in this century, humans will settle on other planets. Our ability to explore and sustain human presence there will not only expand Earth's access to mineral resources but, should the need arise, provide alternative habitats for humanity's survival.

At what cost? Is there a price to inspiration and creativity? Economic, scientific and technological returns of space exploration have far exceeded the investment. Globally, 43 countries now have

---

[2] **Hubble telescope:** a space telescope launched in April of 1990 by the United States, the Hubble telescope orbits Earth and provides clear pictures for astronomical study. It was named for the astronomer Edwin Powell Hubble.

2. **REREAD** Reread lines 15–31. Circle every use of the word *human* in this paragraph. What idea is Vernikos emphasizing by repeating this word? What opposing viewpoint does she refute?

3. **READ** As you read lines 32–55, continue to cite text evidence.

- Circle the questions at the beginning of the first paragraph.
- Underline the claim Vernikos makes about the benefits of space exploration in lines 32–47.
- Underline the claim in lines 48–55 and paraphrase it in the margin.

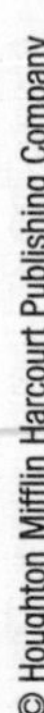

Astronaut Susan L. Still in the Spacelab Module during a mission aboard the Space Shuttle Columbia.

their own observing or communication satellites in Earth orbit. Observing Earth has provided G.P.S.,[3] meteorological forecasts, predictions and management of hurricanes and other natural disasters, and global monitoring of the environment, as well as **surveillance** and intelligence. Satellite communications have changed life and business practices with computer operations, cell phones, global banking, and TV. Studying humans living in the microgravity[4] of space has expanded our understanding of osteoporosis and balance disorders, and has led to new treatments. Wealth-generating medical devices and instrumentation such as digital mammography and outpatient breast biopsy procedures and the application of telemedicine to emergency care are but a few of the social and economic benefits of manned exploration that we take for granted.

surveillance:

Space exploration is not a drain on the economy; it generates infinitely more wealth than it spends. Royalties on NASA patents and licenses currently go directly to the U.S. Treasury, not back to NASA. I firmly believe that the Life Sciences Research Program would be self-supporting if permitted to receive the return on its investment. NASA has done so much with so little that it has generally been assumed to have had a huge budget. In fact, the 2007 NASA budget of $16.3 billion is a minute fraction of the $13 trillion total G.D.P.[5]

[3] **G.P.S.:** an abbreviation for Global Positioning System, a system for determining one's position on Earth by comparing radio signals received from different satellites placed into orbit by the United States Department of Defense (DOD).

[4] **microgravity:** also called *zero gravity* or *weightlessness*, microgravity is the near absence of gravity.

[5] **G.D.P.:** an abbreviation for Gross Domestic Product, the total market value of all the goods and services that are produced inside a country during a specified period.

4. **REREAD AND DISCUSS** With a small group, discuss whether the evidence Vernikos cites to defend the cost of space exploration is sufficient (lines 48–55). Cite text evidence in your discussion.

5. **READ** Read lines 56–67. Underline the opposing viewpoint Vernikos references, and restate it in the margin.

legitimate:

"What's the hurry?" is a **legitimate** question. As the late Senator William Proxmire said many years ago, "Mars isn't going anywhere." Why should we commit hard-pressed budgets for space exploration when there will always be competing interests? However, as Mercury, Gemini and Apollo did 50 years ago, our future scientific and technological leadership depends on exciting creativity in the younger generations. Nothing does this better than manned space exploration. There is now a national urgency to direct the creative interests of our youth towards careers in science and engineering. We need to keep the flame of manned space exploration alive as China, Russia, India, and other countries forge ahead with substantial investments that challenge U.S. leadership in space.

6. REREAD Reread lines 56–67 and continue to cite text evidence.

- Underline the counterargument Vernikos addresses.
- Then circle the pieces of evidence you find most convincing.
- Make notes in the margin to justify your choices.

SHORT RESPONSE

Cite Text Evidence Explain whether or not Vernikos convinced you that space exploration is worth the cost. Review your reading notes, and evaluate the strength and reasonableness of the claims and evidence offered. Be sure to **cite text evidence** from the essay in your response.

Background **Elisabeth Rosenthal** *(born 1956) is a medical doctor and an award-winning journalist. Before Rosenthal was named science editor for the* New York Times, *she worked as a reporter in Beijing, China, where she broke landmark stories on health in China. In this article, she writes about swarms of jellyfish in the waters off the coast of Barcelona, Spain, and explains what their growing numbers tell us about the health of the world's oceans.*

Stinging Tentacles Offer Hint of Oceans' Decline

Newspaper Article by Elisabeth Rosenthal

CLOSE READ Notes

1. READ ▶ As you read lines 1–17, begin to collect and cite evidence.
   - Circle the central idea in the third paragraph, and underline the details that support it.
   - In the margin, restate the central idea of this paragraph.
   - Circle the central idea in lines 15–17, and paraphrase the idea in the margin.

August 3, 2008

BARCELONA, Spain—Blue patrol boats crisscross the swimming areas of beaches here with their huge nets **skimming** the water's surface. The yellow flags that urge caution and the red flags that prohibit swimming because of risky currents are sometimes topped now with blue ones warning of a new danger: swarms of jellyfish.

In a period of hours during a day a couple of weeks ago, 300 people on Barcelona's bustling beaches were treated for stings, and 11 were taken to hospitals.

From Spain to New York, to Australia, Japan and Hawaii, jellyfish are becoming more numerous and more widespread, and they are showing up in places where they have rarely been seen before, scientists say. The faceless marauders are stinging children blithely bathing on summer vacations, forcing beaches to close and clogging fishing nets.

skimming:

But while jellyfish invasions are a nuisance to tourists and a hardship to fishermen, for scientists they are a source of more profound alarm, a signal of the declining health of the world's oceans.

"These jellyfish near shore are a message the sea is sending us saying, 'Look how badly you are treating me,' " said Dr. Josep-María Gili, a leading jellyfish expert, who has studied them at the Institute of Marine Sciences of the Spanish National Research Council in Barcelona for more than 20 years.

The explosion of jellyfish populations, scientists say, reflects a combination of severe overfishing of natural predators, like tuna, sharks and swordfish; rising sea temperatures caused in part by global warming; and pollution that has depleted oxygen levels in coastal shallows.

pronounced:

These problems are **pronounced** in the Mediterranean, a sea bounded by more than a dozen countries that rely on it for business and pleasure. Left unchecked in the Mediterranean and elsewhere, these problems could make the swarms of jellyfish menacing coastlines a grim vision of seas to come.

"The problem on the beach is a social problem," said Dr. Gili, who talks with admiration of the "beauty" of the globular jellyfish. "We need to take care of it for our tourism industry. But the big problem is not on the beach. It's what's happening in the seas."

2. **◀ REREAD** Reread lines 9–17. Review the central ideas in the two paragraphs and write a summary of the text so far. Include essential supporting details.

3. **READ ▶** As you read lines 18–59, analyze the cause-and-effect pattern of organization.

- Circle the causes of events and underline the effects of each cause.
- Record notes in the margin about how one or more events, or causes, bring about one or more other events, or effects.

Jellyfish, relatives of the sea anemone and coral that for the most part are relatively harmless, in fact are the cockroaches of the open waters, the ultimate maritime survivors who thrive in damaged environments, and that is what they are doing.

Within the past year, there have been beach closings because of jellyfish swarms on the Côte d'Azur in France, the Great Barrier Reef of Australia, and at Waikiki in the United States.

In Australia, more than 30,000 people were treated for stings last year, double the number in 2005. The rare but deadly Irukandji jellyfish is expanding its range in Australia's warming waters, marine scientists say.

While no good global database exists on jellyfish populations, the increasing reports from around the world have convinced scientists that the trend is real, serious and climate-related, although they caution that jellyfish populations in any one place undergo year-to-year variation.

"Human-caused stresses, including global warming and overfishing, are encouraging jellyfish surpluses in many tourist destinations and productive fisheries," according to the National Science Foundation, which is issuing a report on the phenomenon this fall and lists as problem areas Australia, the Gulf of Mexico, Hawaii, the Black Sea, Namibia, Britain, the Mediterranean, the Sea of Japan and the Yangtze estuary.

4. **REREAD** Reread Dr. Gili's statements in lines 18–19 and 33–36. Paraphrase his comments in your own words.

CLOSE READ
Notes

> Though the stuff of horror B-movies, jellyfish are hardly aggressors.

In Barcelona, one of Spain's most vibrant tourist destinations, city officials and the Catalan Water Agency have started fighting back, trying desperately to ensure that it is safe for swimmers to go back in the water.

Each morning, with the help of Dr. Gili's team, boats monitor offshore jellyfish swarms, winds and currents to see if beaches are threatened and if closings are needed. They also check if jellyfish collection in the waters near the beaches is needed. Nearly 100 boats stand ready to help in an emergency, said Xavier Duran of the water agency. The constant squeal of Dr. Gili's cellphone reflected his de facto role as Spain's jellyfish control and command center. Calls came from all over.

lethal:

Officials in Santander and the Basque country were concerned about frequent sightings this year on the Atlantic coast of the Portuguese man-of-war, a sometimes **lethal** warm-water species not previously seen regularly in those regions.

Farther south, a fishing boat from the Murcia region called to report an off-shore swarm of Pelagia noctiluca—an iridescent purplish jellyfish that issues a nasty sting—more than a mile long. A

5. READ ▶ As you read lines 60–97, continue to cite evidence.
   - In the margin, list the steps Dr. Gili takes to protect the beaches.
   - Underline the dangers the jellyfish pose for humans.

CLOSE READ
Notes

chef, presumably trying to find some advantage in the declining oceans, wanted to know if the local species were safe to eat if cooked. Much is unknown about the jellyfish, and Dr. Gili was unsure.

In previous decades there were jellyfish problems for only a couple of days every few years; now the threat of jellyfish is a daily headache for local officials and is featured on the evening news. "In the past few years the dynamic has changed completely—the temperature is a little warmer," Dr. Gili said.

Though the stuff of horror B-movies, jellyfish are hardly aggressors. They float haplessly with the currents. They discharge their venom automatically when they bump into something warm—a human body, for example—from poison-containing stingers on mantles, arms or long, threadlike tendrils, which can grow to be yards long.

Some, like the Portuguese man-of-war or the giant box jellyfish, can be deadly on contact. Pelagia noctiluca, common in the Mediterranean, delivers a painful sting producing a wound that lasts weeks, months or years, depending on the person and the amount of contact.

In the Mediterranean, overfishing of both large and small fish has left jellyfish with little competition for plankton, their food, and fewer predators. Unlike in Asia, where some jellyfish are eaten by people, here they have no economic or **epicurean** value.

epicurean:

6. REREAD AND DISCUSS Reread lines 64–86. With a small group, evaluate the efforts of Dr. Gili's team in the struggle to protect the beaches. Is this a long-term solution or a short-term solution to the problem? Cite text evidence in your discussion.

7. READ As you read lines 98–117, continue to cite text evidence.

- Circle the central ideas attributed to Purcell and Gili.
- Then in the margin, summarize what the two experts see as the major causes for the jellyfish invasion.

The warmer seas and drier climate caused by global warming work to the jellyfish's advantage, since nearly all jellyfish breed better and faster in warmer waters, according to Dr. Jennifer Purcell, a jellyfish expert at the Shannon Point Marine Center of Western Washington University.

Global warming has also reduced rainfall in temperate zones, researchers say, allowing the jellyfish to better approach the beaches. Rain runoff from land would normally slightly decrease the salinity of coastal waters, "creating a natural barrier that keeps the jellies from the coast," Dr. Gili said.

Then there is pollution, which reduces oxygen levels and visibility in coastal waters. While other fish die in or avoid waters with low oxygen levels, many jellyfish can thrive in them. And while most fish have to see to catch their food, jellyfish, which filter food passively from the water, can dine in total darkness, according to Dr. Purcell's research.

8. **READ ▶** As you read lines 118–144, continue to cite text evidence.

- Underline what happens to Mirela Gómez after she is stung.
- Underline what Dr. Nogué says about the effect of the stings.
- Circle what Antonio López says about jellyfish.

Residents in Barcelona have forged a prickly coexistence with their new neighbors.

Last month, Mirela Gómez, 8, ran out of the water crying with her first jellyfish sting, clutching a leg that had suddenly become painful and itchy. Her grandparents rushed her to a nearby Red Cross stand. "I'm a little afraid to go back in the water," she said, displaying a row of angry red welts on her shin.

Francisco Antonio Padrós, a 77-year-old fisherman, swore mightily as he unloaded his catch one morning last weekend, pulling off dozens of jellyfish clinging to his nets and tossing them onto a dock. Removing a few shrimp, he said his nets were often "filled with more jellyfish than fish."

By the end of the exercise his calloused hands were bright red and swollen to twice their normal size. "Right now I can't tell if I have hands or not—they hurt, they're numb, they itch," he said.

Dr. Santiago Nogué, head of the **toxicology** unit at the largest hospital here, said that although 90 percent of stings healed in a week or two, many people's still hurt and itched for months. He said he was now seeing 20 patients a year whose symptoms did not respond to any treatment at all, sometimes requiring surgery to remove the affected area.

toxicology:

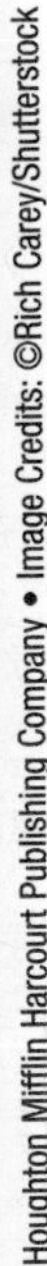

The sea, however, has long been central to life in Barcelona, and that is unlikely to change. Recently when the beaches were closed, children on a breakwater collected jellyfish in a bucket. The next day, Antonio López, a diver, emerged from the water. "There are more every year—we saw hundreds offshore today," he said. "You just have to learn how to handle the stings."

9. **REREAD** Reread lines 139–144. Restate what Antonio López says in your own words.

SHORT RESPONSE

Cite Text Evidence Briefly summarize the growing problem of jellyfish as it is presented in this article. Review your notes, and be sure to **cite text evidence** as you explain the causes and effects of the growing population of jellyfish.

COLLECTION **5**

The Stuff of Consumer Culture

COLLECTION **5**

The Stuff of Consumer Culture

"We live much of our lives in a realm I call the *buyosphere*."

—Thomas Hine

Background *The world's first text message was sent on December 3, 1992. Neil Papworth sent the message "Merry Christmas" from his personal computer to the phone of Richard Jarvis. Technology has come quite a long way since then. The social networking site Facebook has over one billion active users; 2.4 billion people around the world use text messaging as a means of communication; and 30.2 percent of the world's population now use the Internet. Maybe it's important to ask: What are the effects of our obsession with new technology?*

Magazine Article by Andres Padilla-Lopez

1. **READ ▶** As you read lines 1–23, begin to collect and cite text evidence.
   - Underline examples of technology overuse.
   - In the margin, summarize the cause-and-effect relationship found in lines 6–10.
   - In the margin, write what the author is seeking to determine by asking questions (lines 16–23).

Teenage Use of Electronic Devices

Allison, a fifteen-year-old teenager from Redwood City, California, receives more than 27,000 text messages a month. This averages out to about 900 texts per day. Allison explains, "I text while I'm doing like *everything*. . . . I *need* to answer that text. I need to know who's talking to me, to know what they're going to say."

Another teenager, also from Redwood City, spends six to seven hours a day playing video games. He admits that his game playing has interfered with his grades. But, he argues that video games "give me a shot of energy" and "playing just makes me happy . . . I can't stop playing them. I don't want to stop playing them."

In an interview with a British reporter, one teenager said with feeling, "I'd rather give up a kidney than my phone." Another told the same reporter that she spends over an hour on school days and about

The kid like playing video games because it gives him a shot of energy. But the Effect is that his grades drop

He is seeking to determine why teens use so much time on their devices

double that time on weekends hanging out with some 450 Facebook friends.

So, how do *you* use electronic devices? Are your Facebook friends the same as your real-life friends, or do they include people you've never met? Are the friends you've never met more interesting than your real-life friends? Do you feel lost without your cell phone? Must you answer every text message immediately? Are you itching to get out of class to play video games? Or perhaps you worry about the amount of time you spend on your electronic devices. Maybe you think that texting and Facebook are a waste of time.

Facts and Figures

Recent studies estimate that 93 percent of teenagers between the ages of 12 and 17 years of age regularly go online to use the Internet. Studies also show that 75 percent of all teenagers own cell phones. Half of that 75 percent sends fifty or more texts a day. One in three sends 100 or more texts per day. Some teenage cellphone users don't even use their phones to make actual phone calls—except to their

2. REREAD Reread lines 1–15. What are the similarities of the structure of each of the first three paragraphs? Support your response with explicit textual evidence.

3. READ As you read lines 24–35 and study the bar graphs, continue to cite evidence.

- Underline text that contains numerical data, and circle text that makes a generalization. In the margin, note a difference between these two kinds of information.
- What conclusion can you draw about landline phones from the information in the graphs? Note your conclusion in the margin.
- In the margin, make an inference about the reason teenagers may make "actual phone calls" to their parents.

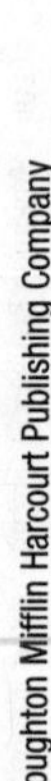

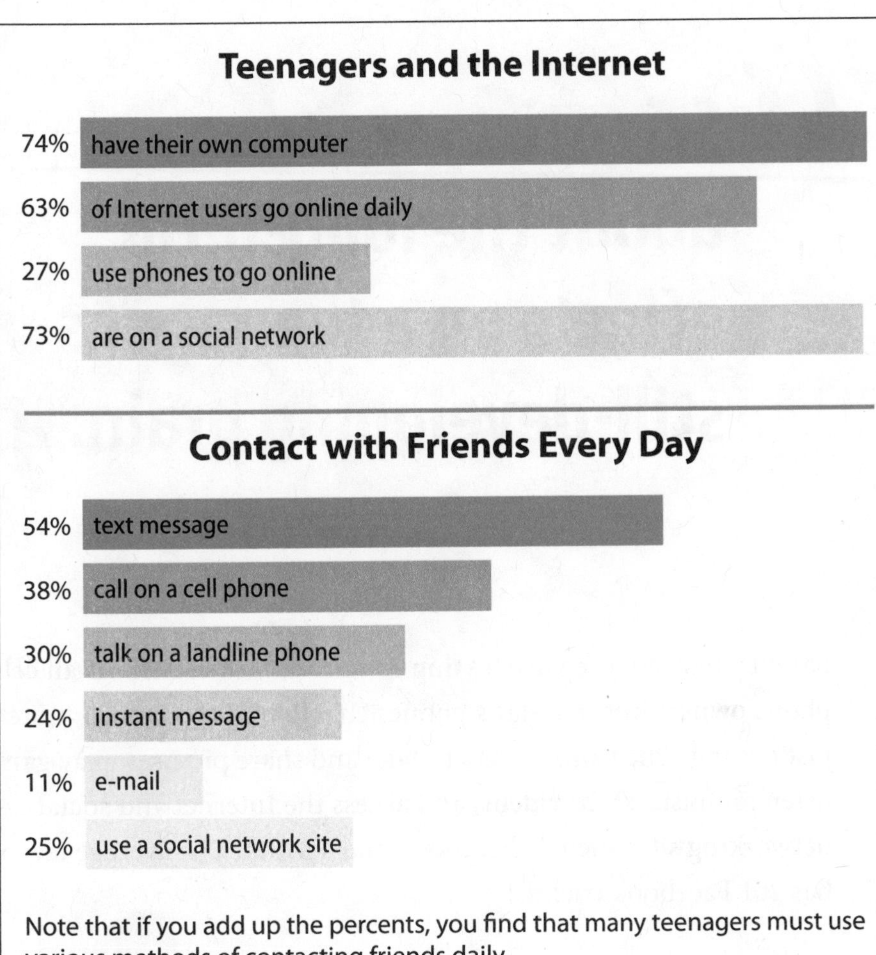

4. REREAD Review the graphs. What conclusion can you draw about why significantly more teenagers use text messaging than e-mail to communicate with their friends? Support your answer with explicit evidence from the graphs.

more teenagers text there friends because we may not have our friends personaly email so we text them and it much eaiser if i have my phone right next to me

> **“Scientists wonder about the long-term effects on a teenager’s still-developing brain.”**

The author seems to be on the con side he brings up a lot negative things

parents. Instead, they use texting to communicate. And, as all cell phone owners know, today’s phones enable you to do much more than just texting. They allow users to take and share pictures, play games, listen to music, swap videos, and access the Internet and social networking sites such as Facebook and Twitter. The average teenager has 201 Facebook friends!

The Pros and the Cons

aptly:

One high school student from California **aptly** sums up the conflicting attitudes held by both adults and teenagers about the use of digital devices. Vishal is a bright seventeen-year old with a passionate interest in filmmaking. As he puts it, technology is “bad for me as a student” because it has caused his grades to go down. On the other hand, he says, it is “good for me as a learner.” Vishal’s access to technology has distracted him and made it difficult for him to concentrate on his assigned schoolwork, but it has also helped him to pursue in depth his interest in filmmaking.

Currently educators, scientists, parents, and even some teenagers themselves worry about the long-term effects of always being

5. **READ ▶** As you read lines 36–57, continue to cite textual evidence.

- Underline negative effects of using digital devices.
- Circle positive effects of using digital devices.
- In the margin, explain what positions, pro or con, the author seems to emphasize.

connected to electronic devices. Educators notice a decline in students' ability to concentrate on any one thing for an extended period of time. Scientists wonder about the long-term effects on a teenager's still-developing brain. What do the instant **gratification** and rapid stimulation offered by electronic media do to a teenager's brain? Scientists also fear that yielding to one distraction after another develops an inability to focus. Parents worry about the presence of predators on social networking sites. They are also alarmed by the threat of cyber-bullying. Teenagers, like Vishal and Allison, ask themselves if their slipping grades and inability to concentrate on school tasks are worth it.

On the other hand, supporters argue that today's powerful cell phones offer teenagers new worlds of opportunity. They stress that understanding new technology is essential to future success. They recognize that tools, such as texting and Facebook, meet needs common to all teenagers, such as defining their personal identity and establishing their independence. These technologies provide new avenues for teenagers to do the things teenagers have always wanted to do: flirt, boast, gossip, complain, tease, and get news. Some educators see new technologies as an exciting way of connecting with students. Others view them as a tool for personalizing education and encouraging individual students' interests.

gratification:

The author seems to put a lot mor positive things in this

6. REREAD Reread lines 36–57. Explain how the cause-and-effect pattern of organization is used in this section to connect ideas. Support your answer with explicit textual evidence.

7. READ As you read lines 58–71, continue to cite textual evidence.

- Circle positive effects of using digital devices.
- In the margin, explain which position, pro or con, the author emphasizes now.

Wherever you stand on the various issues raised, there is no doubt that electronic devices are here to stay. How we use these devices, whether we choose to have them work for us or against us, is up to us.

8. **REREAD AND DISCUSS** Reread lines 58–71. With a small group, draw several conclusions about the ways that teens can use technological devices to work for them instead of against them. Cite explicit textual evidence in your discussion.

SHORT RESPONSE

Cite Text Evidence What types of information does the author include to show the ways in which teens use technological devices? What overall insight does the reader gain on the use of these devices? Review your reading notes, and be sure to **cite evidence from the text** in your response.

The author includes how teens text and gain information from there devicis line 30. The reader gains how some teens use the devices and how others use this as a platform of learning and gaining information line 40 + 60

Background *Obesity is a leading cause of preventable death in America. Between the 1980s and the 2000s, childhood obesity rates tripled in the United States. This increase can be directly attributed to an increase in snacking and portion sizes and a decrease in physical activity. Children who are obese are significantly more likely to be obese as adults. A nationwide initiative to combat obesity through education and a focus on increasing physical activity may hold the key to battling this epidemic.*

Labels and Illusions

Essay by Lourdes Barranco

1. **READ ▶** As you read lines 1–17, begin to cite text evidence.
   - Underline phrases that describe what marketers do.
   - In the margin, make an inference about the effect of certain marketing strategies on obesity.

Let's face it, these days we all are worried about the expanding size of American waistlines. Some of us worry about our own waistlines; others are concerned with the rise in obesity among Americans in general. One thing we should examine more closely is how marketers—the people who **devise** strategies to make us buy certain products—are contributing to the rise of obesity in our country.

devise:

Marketers have developed some fanciful food labeling strategies to make us think we are consuming less food, when in fact we are not. For example, you might order a medium soft drink in a fast food restaurant (seemingly a wise move if you're trying to eat less). You later discover that the same size soft drink has magically transformed itself into a "large" drink in another restaurant. Which size soda did you actually drink: a medium or a large? Perhaps you ask for a small order of french fries in a restaurant, and when you get it, it seems huge. The labeling of these food and drink items seems whimsical, if not completely inaccurate. What's going on?

For those of us trying to eat reasonable portions, an additional problem can arise from our own inability to judge the size of our meals. Consider the following optical illusion, first documented in 1875: the Delboeuf [del bœf] effect. Start with two dots of equal size. Then surround one dot with a large circle and the other with a small circle. Guess what happens—suddenly the second dot, the one surrounded by the small circle, looks much larger than the first dot, even though they are the same size.

What does this have to do with the amount of food we eat? Koert van Ittersum, a professor of marketing at Georgia Tech, and Brian Wansink, director of the Food and Brand Lab at Cornell, found out. They performed a series of experiments to measure the effect of the Delboeuf illusion on people's perception of portion size. They served two groups of people the same size portion but on different-size plates. People who were served on larger plates thought that they had been served a small portion. People served on smaller plates thought that they had been served a large portion. The research showed that

2. **◀ REREAD** Reread lines 8–17. A contrast between what is expected and what actually occurs is called *irony*. The use of irony can create strong effects, including humor. What words and phrases add an ironic tone to this paragraph?

3. **READ ▶** As you read lines 18–36, continue to cite textual evidence.

- Underline the results of each experiment.
- In the margin, explain how the results of the Delboeuf effect compare to those of the van Ittersum/Wansink experiment.

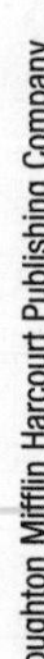

our eyes can deceive us about the amount of food we're actually eating.

To make the problem worse, marketers working in the clothing industry have created strategies for making us think that we are thinner than we actually are. A common dilemma faced by people of all ages is trying to determine which size of an article of clothing fits them. Their confusion is understandable. Depending on the store, a pair of slacks labeled size 8, 6, or 4 might fit the same woman. A sweater labeled extra large or medium might fit a large man.

What causes these differences? The answer is "vanity sizing," the practice of labeling clothes as smaller sizes than they really are. In other words, a dress that is really a size 8 may be labeled a size 2. By using vanity sizing, clothing manufacturers flatter people into thinking that they are not as large as they may actually be. Apparently, this encourages people to purchase the items of clothing. Remember, the marketers who devise these labels are people who want you to buy their company's products.

4. **◀ REREAD** Reread lines 18–36. State the main idea of this section and explain how both experiments support it.

5. **READ ▶** As you read lines 37–58, continue to cite textual evidence.

- Underline phrases that suggest that "vanity sizing" makes people feel good.
- Circle the conclusion that sums up the central idea of this essay.
- In the margin, restate what consumers can do to counteract the influence of marketers.

What can consumers do? First, we should ignore the labels "small," "medium," and "large" as they apply to food and drink. We're probably buying a lot more than we need. We should also be skeptical of clothing labels. We may not be as trim and physically fit as the label would lead us to believe. To stay healthy and avoid obesity, we must rely on our own good sense and on our knowledge of what characterizes a healthy person.

6. REREAD Reread lines 52–58. An author may use more than one kind of tone in an essay. What word would you use to describe the author's tone in this paragraph? What words and phrases reflect this tone?

SHORT RESPONSE

Cite Text Evidence Summarize the central idea of this essay and the most effective information the author includes to support it. **Cite text evidence** and relevant reading notes in your response.

Background Shinichi Hoshi *(1926–1997) is well-known in Japan for his quirky imagination and intriguing science fiction stories. Hoshi wrote more than 1,000 short stories. He is most famous for his "short short" stories—many only three or four pages long. This story takes place in a Japanese fishing village. Japan boasts one of the largest fish catches in the world. However, Japanese waters are plagued by pollution and environmental problems.*

He—y, Come On Ou—t!

Short Story by Shinichi Hoshi

1. **READ ▶** As you read lines 1–30, begin to cite text evidence.
   - Circle the important events described in lines 1–4.
   - Underline details that describe the hole. In the margin, list things that seem odd about the hole.
   - Circle significant statements in lines 21–28.

The **typhoon** had passed and the sky was a gorgeous blue. Even a certain village not far from the city had suffered damage. A little distance from the village and near the mountains, a small shrine had been swept away by a landslide.

typhoon:

"I wonder how long that shrine's been here."

"Well, in any case, it must have been here since an awfully long time ago."

"We've got to rebuild it right away."

While the villagers exchanged views, several more of their number came over.

"It sure was wrecked."

"I think it used to be right here."

"No, looks like it was a little more over there."

Just then one of them raised his voice. "Hey what in the world is this hole?"

Where they had all gathered there was a hole about a meter in diameter. They peered in, but it was so dark nothing could be seen. However, it gave one the feeling that it was so deep it went clear through to the center of the earth.

There was even one person who said, "I wonder if it's a fox's hole."

"He—y, come on ou—t!" shouted a young man into the hole. There was no echo from the bottom. Next he picked up a pebble and was about to throw it in.

"You might bring down a curse on us. Lay off," warned an old man, but the younger one energetically threw the pebble in. As before, however, there was no answering response from the bottom. The villagers cut down some trees, tied them with rope and made a fence which they put around the hole. Then they repaired to the village.

"What do you suppose we ought to do?"

"Shouldn't we build the shrine up just as it was over the hole?"

A day passed with no agreement. The news traveled fast, and a car from the newspaper company rushed over. In no time a scientist came out, and with an all-knowing expression on his face he went over to the hole. Next, a bunch of gawking curiosity seekers showed up; one could also pick out here and there men of shifty glances who appeared to be **concessionaires**. Concerned that someone might fall into the hole, a policeman from the local substation kept a careful watch.

concessionaire:

One newspaper reporter tied a weight to the end of a long cord and lowered it into the hole. A long way down it went. The cord ran out, however, and he tried to pull it out, but it would not come back up. Two or three people helped out, but when they all pulled too hard, the cord parted at the edge of the hole. Another reporter, a camera in

2. REREAD Reread lines 1–30. Which details about the setting seem realistic? Which details suggest an otherworldly setting?

3. READ As you read lines 31–74, continue to cite text evidence.

- Circle the sentences that show the scientist's thoughts.
- In the margin, paraphrase the significant statement in line 58.
- Underline the concessionaire's offers to the mayor in lines 59–68.

hand, who had been watching all of this, quietly untied a stout rope that had been wound around his waist.

The scientist contacted people at his laboratory and had them bring out a high-powered bull horn, with which he was going to check out the echo from the hole's bottom. He tried switching through various sounds, but there was no echo. The scientist was puzzled, but he could not very well give up with everyone watching him so intently. He put the bull horn right up to the hole, turned it to its highest volume, and let it sound continuously for a long time. It was a noise that would have carried several dozen kilometers above ground. But the hole just calmly swallowed up the sound.

In his own mind the scientist was at a loss, but with a look of apparent **composure** he cut off the sound and, in a manner suggesting that the whole thing had a perfectly plausible explanation, said simply, "Fill it in."

composure:

Safer to get rid of something one didn't understand.

The onlookers, disappointed that this was all that was going to happen, prepared to disperse. Just then one of the concessionaires, having broken through the throng and come forward, made a proposal.

"Let me have that hole. I'll fill it in for you."

"We'd be grateful to you for filling it in," replied the mayor of the village, "but we can't very well give you the hole. We have to build a shrine there."

"If it's a shrine you want, I'll build you a fine one later. Shall I make it with an attached meeting hall?"

Before the mayor could answer, the people of the village all shouted out.

“Really? Well, in that case, we ought to have it closer to the village.”

“It’s just an old hole. We’ll give it to you!”

So it was settled. And the mayor, of course, had no objection.

The concessionaire was true to his promise. It was small, but closer to the village he did build for them a shrine with an attached meeting hall.

About the time the autumn festival was held at the new shrine, the hole-filling company established by the concessionaire hung out its small shingle at a shack near the hole.

The concessionaire had his cohorts mount a loud campaign in the city. “We’ve got a fabulously deep hole! Scientists say it’s at least five thousand meters deep! Perfect for the disposal of such things as waste from nuclear reactors.”

consent:

Government authorities granted permission. Nuclear power plants fought for contracts. The people of the village were a bit worried about this, but they **consented** when it was explained that there would be absolutely no above-ground contamination for several thousand years and that they would share in the profits. Into the bargain, very shortly a magnificent road was built from the city to the village.

Trucks rolled in over the road, transporting lead boxes. Above the hole the lids were opened, and the wastes from nuclear reactors tumbled away into the hole.

4. **REREAD** Certain statements in a story will hint at a theme. What theme is suggested by the statement you paraphrased in line 58?

5. **READ** As you read lines 75–136, continue to cite textual evidence.

- Underline all the things that people throw into the hole.
- Make notes in the margin about how the hole is affecting people’s behavior.
- Circle details in lines 126–136 that recall an episode earlier in the story.

CLOSE READ
Notes

From the Foreign Ministry and the Defense Agency boxes of unnecessary classified documents were brought for disposal. Officials who came to supervise the disposal held discussions on golf. The lesser functionaries, as they threw in the papers, chatted about pinball.

The hole showed no signs of filling up. It was awfully deep, thought some; or else it might be very spacious at the bottom. Little by little the hole-filling company expanded its business.

Bodies of animals used in contagious disease experiments at the universities were brought out, and to these were added the unclaimed corpses of vagrants. Better than dumping all of its garbage in the ocean, went the thinking in the city, and plans were made for a long pipe to carry it to the hole.

The hole gave peace of mind to the dwellers of the city. They concentrated solely on producing one thing after another. Everyone disliked thinking about the eventual consequences. People wanted only to work for production companies and sales corporations; they had no interest in becoming junk dealers. But, it was thought, these problems too would gradually be resolved by the hole.

Young girls whose betrothals had been arranged discarded old diaries in the hole. There were also those who were inaugurating new love affairs and threw into the hole old photographs of themselves taken with former sweethearts. The police felt comforted as they used the hole to get rid of accumulations of expertly done **counterfeit** bills. Criminals breathed easier after throwing material evidence into the hole.

counterfeit:

Whatever one wished to discard, the hole accepted it all. The hole cleansed the city of its filth; the sea and sky seemed to have become a bit clearer than before.

Aiming at the heavens, new buildings went on being constructed one after the other.

One day, atop the high steel frame of a new building under construction, a workman was taking a break. Above his head he heard a voice shout:

"He—y, come on ou—t!"

But, in the sky to which he lifted his gaze there was nothing at all. A clear blue sky merely spread over all. He thought it must be his imagination. Then, as he resumed his former position, from the direction where the voice had come, a small pebble skimmed by him and fell on past.

The man, however, was gazing in idle reverie at the city's skyline growing ever more beautiful, and he failed to notice.

6. **◀ REREAD AND DISCUSS** Reread lines 126–136. With a small group, discuss your interpretation of the story's ending. Review your reading notes and cite text evidence in your discussion.

SHORT RESPONSE

Cite Text Evidence A story's theme is the central idea about life that the writer conveys. What is the theme of "He—y, Come On Ou—t!"? Review your reading notes and **cite text evidence** in your response.

COLLECTION **6**

Guided by a Cause

COLLECTION **6**

Guided by a Cause

"The fullness of our heart comes in our actions."

—Mother Teresa

HISTORY WRITING

from "The Most Daring of [Our] Leaders"

Lynne Olson

SPEECH

Speech from the Democratic National Convention

John Lewis

SHORT STORY

Doris Is Coming

ZZ Packer

NEWSPAPER ARTICLE

Difference Maker: John Bergmann and Popcorn Park

David Karas

Background *From the 1880s until the 1960s, "Jim Crow" laws in many American states enforced segregation between white people and black people. When the U.S. Supreme Court overturned the "separate but equal" doctrine in 1954, it was the beginning of a period of upheaval and marked the beginning of the civil rights movement. Civil rights activists participated in nonviolent forms of protest, such as sit-ins at lunch counters, and engaged in acts of civil disobedience, such as riding buses into the Deep South to challenge segregation at interstate terminals.*

from

"The Most Daring of [Our] Leaders"

By Lynne Olson

Speech from the

Democratic National Convention

By John Lewis

Lynne Olson *writes books of nonfiction. Before she started writing books full-time, she worked as a journalist for the Associated Press and as the White House correspondent for the* Baltimore Sun. *Her book* Freedom's Daughters *was the first book to take an in-depth look at women's roles in the civil rights movement. The portion of* Freedom's Daughters *that you will read here tells of the experiences of Diane Nash, a young woman from Chicago who attended Fisk University in Nashville, Tennessee, in 1959. In Nashville, both Diane Nash and John Lewis were influenced by Reverend James Lawson's teachings on the philosophy of nonviolence.*

John Lewis *was born in Alabama in 1940. He was a student at Fisk University when the civil rights movement gained momentum. As a college student, he studied the philosophy of nonviolence. In 1960, he helped plan a lunch counter sit-in in Nashville that went on peacefully for a month and then ended in the beating and arrest of the protesters. Eventually these protests were successful, and Nashville became the first major city in the South to desegregate its lunch counters. Lewis has served as the U.S. Representative of Georgia's Fifth Congressional District since his election to Congress in 1986. In his Speech to the Democratic National Convention, delivered in Charlotte, North Carolina, in 2012, Lewis talks about the progress America has made since he made an earlier trip to Charlotte in 1961.*

1. READ ▶ As you read lines 1–55, begin to collect and cite text evidence.

- Underline Nash's and the Fisk students' reactions to segregation. Explain in the margin how the other students' reactions influenced Nash.
- In the margin, note the central idea of the section. Circle three details that support the main idea.

from "The Most Daring of [Our] Leaders"

History Writing by Lynne Olson

epiphany:

Nash's moment of **epiphany** came at the Tennessee State Fair in 1959. She had gone to the fair on a date, and wanted to use the ladies' room. She found two—one marked WHITE WOMEN, the other COLORED WOMEN—and for the first time in her life suffered the degradation of Jim Crow. This was no longer an intellectual exercise: She was being told in the most searing way imaginable that *she* was beyond the pale, unfit to use the same facilities as white women. Outraged by the experience, she was even more upset that her date, a Southerner, did not share her fury. Neither did most of her fellow Fisk students. They did not seem to care that they could shop at downtown stores but not eat at the stores' lunch counters, or that they had to sit in the balcony to see a movie. The more Nash found out about segregation in Nashville, the more she felt "stifled and boxed in." In the rest of the country, Nashville had the reputation of being more racially progressive than most Southern cities. Blacks could vote in Nashville. The city's schools and buses were integrated. Blacks served on the police force, fire department, City Council, and Board of Education. But segregation still firmly ruled in theaters, restaurants, hotels, and libraries, and Diane Nash, a deep-dyed moralist, decided then and there that Nashville was in a "stage of sin." She couldn't believe that "the children of my classmates would have to be born into a society where they had to believe that they were inferior." Above all, she could not believe that her classmates were willing to let that happen.

Since they did not seem to share her anger, she looked elsewhere for support. Paul LaPrad, a white exchange student at Fisk, told her about a black minister named James Lawson, who was training college students in the use of nonviolence as the framework for an all-out attack on segregation. For Lawson, who had spent three years in India studying the principles of Gandhi, nonviolence was more than just a protest technique: It was the means by which he ordered his life. The young minister talked about the power of nonviolent confrontation with evil, about overcoming the forces of hate and transforming society through love and forgiveness. At first, Nash was skeptical. How could such high-flown idealism be harnessed as a weapon against gun-toting sheriffs and club-swinging racists? Even after attending several of Lawson's workshops, she still was sure "this stuff is never going to work." But since, as she said, it was "the only game in town," she kept going back, and after weeks of studying theology and philosophy, of reading Thoreau and other advocates of passive resistance, of discussion and arguments with the workshop's other participants, the intense young woman from Chicago was finally captured by Lawson's vision. She was particularly drawn to his belief that to be effective, these young would-be activists would have to transcend self-hatred and a sense of inferiority, that they would have to learn to love themselves. Having been raised in a **milieu** that downplayed her blackness, she now found herself part of a group "suddenly proud to be called 'black.' Within the movement . . . we came to a realization of our own worth . . ."

milieu:

In the late fall of 1959, the students at Lawson's workshops formed a central committee to act as the decision-making body for the group. Nash, who had impressed everyone with her clear-eyed thinking and the intensity of her developing commitment to nonviolence, was named to the committee. More and more, the students were turning to her as one of their main leaders.

2. **REREAD** Reread lines 26–49. Why was Nash drawn to the idea of the activists learning "to love themselves"? Support your answer with explicit textual evidence.

> "What am I *doing*? And how is this little group of students my age going to stand up to these powerful people?"

The committee had chosen the lunch counters and restaurants of Nashville's downtown stores as the target of the students' first protest, scheduled for February 1960. For the next several months, the students underwent rigorous training to prepare for the upcoming sit-ins, and on February 13, 124 students left a Nashville church and made their way to the lunch counters of several downtown stores. There, they took their seats and asked for service. The men wore suits and ties, the women, dresses, stockings, and high heels. They were poised and polite and gave little outward sign of the fear many of them felt. Diane Nash, for one, was terrified—a terror that would never leave her, no matter how many sit-ins and protests she would participate in afterward.

As frightened as the students were during that first sit-in, however, they had to struggle to keep from laughing at the stunned, panicky reactions of white store workers and **patrons**, who acted, Nash recalled, as if these well-dressed young people were "some dreadful monster . . . about to devour them all." Waitresses dropped dishes, cashiers broke down in tears, an elderly white woman almost had a seizure when she opened the door of a store's "white" ladies' room and found two young black women inside.

patron:

3. READ ▷ As you read lines 56–106, continue to cite textual evidence.

- Underline activists' preparations and actions in the sit-ins.
- Circle how white store workers, patrons, and the city reacted to the sit-ins.
- In the margin, summarize why Nash was made the head of the committee.
- In the margin, explain how this section is organized.

There were no arrests and no violence. After a couple of hours, the students left the stores, jubilant that their first foray had gone without a hitch. A second sit-in was planned for the following week. In the meantime, several members of the students' Central Committee came to Nash and asked her to head the group. She was hardworking and outwardly fearless, and she did not seem to have the ego problems that a lot of the men had. "Because she was a woman and not a man, I think Diane never had to go around and do any posturing," said Bernard Lafayette, an American Baptist College student and one of the Nashville movement's leaders. But Nash had no desire to become the recognized head of this movement. Like most young women of that time, she had been raised to stay in the background. The men pressured her into accepting, however, and when she returned to her dorm room, she was so frightened by what she had done that she could hardly keep her legs from collapsing under her. "This is Tennessee," she told herself. "We are going to be coming up against . . . white Southern men who are forty and fifty and sixty years old, who are politicians and judges and owners of businesses, and I am twenty-two years old. What am I *doing*? And how is this little group of students my age going to stand up to these powerful people?"

Once again, she managed to damp down her fear. She joined the other students in the second sit-in, which was as quietly successful as the first. Nevertheless, the city was losing its patience. Nashville officials, deluged by complaints from store owners that the sit-ins were causing whites to stay away from downtown, warned the students not to continue. If the warning wasn't heeded, they made clear, the kids could forget about being treated with kid gloves any longer. Worried about the possibility of violence and arrests, the ministers connected with the movement urged the students to reconsider their plans for another demonstration on February 27.

4. **◀ REREAD AND DISCUSS** Reread lines 56–67. In a small group, discuss why the students prepared so intensely for the sit-ins, and why they dressed up for the first protest.

5. **READ ▶** As you read lines 107–123, continue to cite textual evidence. Underline police actions in the February 27 demonstration.

CLOSE READ
Notes

With their numbers swelling, the young people refused. In the middle of another snowstorm, more than three hundred of them poured into downtown Nashville. No sooner had some of them sat down at the Woolworth's lunch counter than the ministers' fears proved justified. The demonstrators were met by an opposing force of cursing young white toughs, who yanked them from their stools and threw them to the floor, beat them with fists and clubs, kicked them, spat on them, extinguished lighted cigarettes on their backs and in their hair. The police were nowhere in sight, and when they finally arrived, they approached not the white attackers, but the bruised and shaken demonstrators, who were spattered with mustard and ketchup, spit and blood. "Okay, get up from the lunch counter or we're going to arrest you," one of the cops barked. When no one obeyed, the students were ordered to their feet, arrested for disorderly conduct, and marched out, through a gauntlet of hostile whites, to police paddy wagons. When they looked over their shoulders at the lunch counter, they saw a new wave of students quietly moving in to take their place.

6. **REREAD** Reread lines 107–123. Explain why the "ministers' fears proved justified" during the sit-in at the Woolworth's lunch counter. In what respect could this sit-in be regarded as a victory? Support your response with explicit textual evidence.

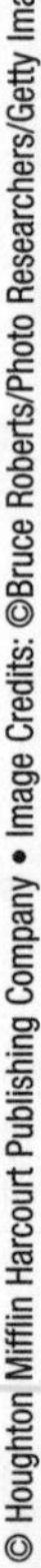

7. **READ ▶** As you read lines 1–44 of John Lewis's speech, continue to cite textual evidence.

- Underline what happened when the Freedom Riders got off the buses, and note in the margin what you can infer about their journey (lines 1–16).
- In the margin, explain the parallels between the Freedom Riders and voting.

Speech from the Democratic National Convention

Speech by John Lewis

I first came to this city in 1961, the year Barack Obama was born. I was one of the 13 original "Freedom Riders." We were on a bus ride from Washington to New Orleans trying to test a recent Supreme Court ruling that banned racial discrimination on buses crossing state lines and in the stations that served them. Here in Charlotte, a young African-American rider got off the bus and tried to get a shoe shine in a so-called white waiting room. He was arrested and taken to jail.

On that same day, we continued on to Rock Hill, South Carolina, about 25 miles. From here, when my seatmate, Albert Bigelow, and I tried to enter a white waiting room, we were met by an angry mob that beat us and left us lying in a pool of blood. Some police officers came up and asked us whether we wanted to press charges. We said, "No, we come in peace, love and nonviolence." We said our struggle was not against individuals, but against unjust laws and customs. Our goal was true freedom for every American.

Since then, America has made a lot of progress. We are a different society than we were in 1961. And in 2008, we showed the world the true promise of America when we elected President Barack Obama. A few years ago, a man from Rock Hill, inspired by President Obama's election, decided to come forward. He came to my office in Washington and said, "I am one of the people who beat you. I want to apologize. Will you forgive me?" I said, "I accept your apology." He started crying. He gave me a hug. I hugged him back, and we both started crying. This man and I don't want to go back; we want to move forward.

Brothers and sisters, do you want to go back? Or do you want to keep America moving forward? My dear friends, your vote is precious, almost sacred. It is the most powerful, nonviolent tool we have to create a more perfect union. Not too long ago, people stood in unmovable lines. They had to pass a so-called literacy test, pay a poll tax. On one occasion, a man was asked to count the number of bubbles in a bar of soap. On another occasion, one was asked to count the jelly beans in a jar—all to keep them from casting their ballots.

Today it is unbelievable that there are officials still trying to stop some people from voting. They are changing the rules, cutting polling hours and imposing requirements intended to suppress the vote.

I've seen this before. I've lived this before. Too many people struggled, suffered and died to make it possible for every American to exercise their right to vote.

And we have come too far together to ever turn back. So we must not be silent. We must stand up, speak up and speak out. We must march to the polls like never before. We must come together and exercise our sacred right.

8. **REREAD AND DISCUSS** Reread lines 17–26. With a small group, discuss the anecdote Lewis relates about the man from Rock Hill. In what way did this incident allow both men "to move forward"? Cite text evidence in your discussion.

SHORT RESPONSE

Cite Text Evidence Compare and contrast the texts by Olson and Lewis. What is similar and different in the two accounts? Review your reading notes and be sure to **cite text evidence** in your response.

Background ZZ Packer *(born 1973) is an award-winning writer of short fiction. She nicknamed herself ZZ because her given name, Zuwena (Swahili for "good"), was hard for teachers to pronounce. Recognized as a talent at an early age, Packer's first significant publication was in* Seventeen *magazine, when she was 19. "Doris Is Coming" is a short story about a young African American girl growing up Louisville, Kentucky, in the early 1960s.*

Doris Is Coming

Short Story by ZZ Packer

CLOSE READ
Notes

1. **READ ▶** As you read lines 1–23, begin to collect and cite text evidence.

- Underline parts of the text that describe the setting.
- In the margin, summarize what the main character is doing in lines 1–14.
- In the margin, note the conflict that arises in lines 15–23.

She walked from Stutz's and up along Fourth Street. When she got to Claremont, the street where she lived, she kept going, past Walnut and Chestnut and all the other streets named after trees. She hit the little business district, which was still lit for New Year's, the big incandescent bulbs on wires like buds growing from vines, entwining the trees and lighting the shop facades. When she walked farther, she felt, for the first time, some purpose other than solitude motivating her. She rushed, and did not know why, until she found it, Clovee's Five and Dime. As soon as she saw it, she knew what she was doing.

It was warm inside, and she made her way to the soda fountain, even warmer from the grill's heat. A white man stood at the ice cream machine and whirred a shake. Two white men sat at the counter and talked in low, serious tones, occasionally sucking up clots of shake through a straw.

There was one waitress, hip propped against the side of the counter, wiping the countertop with a rag that had seen cleaner days. Without looking up she said, "Sorry. We don't serve colored people."

"Good." Doris said. "I don't eat them." She remembered Helen telling her that this was the line someone used during a sit-in, and Doris was glad to have a chance to use it.

The waitress frowned, confused, but when she finally got it, she laughed. "Seriously though," the waitress said, turning solemn. "I can't serve you."

The two men talking looked over at her and shook their heads. They began talking again, occasionally looking over at Doris to see if she'd left.

"What if I stay?"

The waitress looked to the man making the shake, eyes pleading for help. "I don't know. I don't know. I just don't make the rules and I feel sorry for you, but I don't make 'em."

The man walked over with a shake and gave it to the waitress, who bent the straw toward herself and began to drink it. "Look," the man said to Doris, "I wouldn't sit here. I wouldn't do that."

"You wouldn't?"

"I wouldn't if I were you."

She sat. Shaking, she brought out her World History book. She'd made a book cover for it with a paper bag, and she was glad she'd done it because she was sweating so much it would have slipped from her hands otherwise. She set it on the counter, opened it, as if she did this everyday at this very shop, and tried to read about the Hapsburgs, but couldn't.

It occurred to her that other students who did sit-ins were all smarter than she; they'd banded together, and had surely told others

2. ◀ **REREAD AND DISCUSS** With a small group, discuss Doris's "joke"—what it means, what it tells you about Doris, and how it advances the plot (lines 15–23).

3. **READ** ▶ As you read lines 24–47, continue to cite textual evidence.

- Circle the actions that reveal Doris's feelings.
- Underline what the waitress and the man say to Doris.
- In the margin, summarize the developing situation.

CLOSE READ Notes

of their whereabouts, whereas she had foolishly come to Clovee's all by herself. She stared at her book and didn't dare look up, but from the corner of her eye she noticed when the two men who'd been talking got up and left.

The man at the ice cream machine made himself some coffee and beckoned the waitress to him. When he whispered something to her, she swatted him with the rag, laughing.

Once Doris felt the numbness settle in her, she felt she could do it. She tried at the Hapsburgs again.

The waitress said, "Student? High school?"

"Yes, Ma'am. Central."

"My daughter's over at Iroquois."

"We played them last Friday." Doris didn't know what the scores were, didn't care, but had heard about the game over the intercom.

"Well." The waitress started wiping the counter again. Going over the same spots.

When Doris closed her book, about to leave, she said, "I just want you to know I'm leaving now. Not because you're making me or because I feel **intimidated** or anything. I just have to go home now."

intimidate:

The waitress looked at her.

"Next time I'll want some food, all right?"

"We can't do that, but here's half my shake. You can have it. I'm done."

The shake she handed over had a lipstick ring around the straw, and a little spittle. Doris knew she wouldn't drink it, but she took it anyway. "Thanks, ma'am."

4. **◀ REREAD** Reread lines 42–47. What mistake does Doris see she's made? Cite text evidence in your answer.

5. **READ ▶** As you read lines 48–79, continue to cite textual evidence.

- In the margin, explain the connection the waitress makes with Doris.
- Circle details that show Doris is in control of her actions and emotions.
- In the margin, make an inference about how Doris feels about her experience (lines 70–79).

Outside Clovee's Five and Dime, the world was cold around her, moving toward dark, but not dark yet, as if the darkness were being adjusted with a volume dial. Whoever was adjusting the dial was doing it slowly, consistently, with infinite patience. She walked back home and knew it would be too late for dinner, and the boys would be screaming and her father wanting his daily beer, and her mother worried sick. She knew that she should hurry, but she couldn't. She had to stop and look. The sky had just turned her favorite shade of barely lit blue, the kind that came to windows when you couldn't get back to sleep but couldn't quite pry yourself awake.

6. **REREAD** Reread lines 51–79. How have the characters' perspectives changed? Cite explicit textual evidence in your response.

SHORT RESPONSE

Cite Text Evidence Think about the texts in this Collection that describe the real experiences of Diane Nash and John Lewis during sit-ins in the 1960s. What references to historical details do you find in the story? In what ways are Doris's fictional experiences different from the real experiences of Nash and Lewis? **Cite text evidence** in your response.

Background *Every year, millions of pets are taken in by animal shelters. You may even know someone whose pet was adopted from a shelter. But what happens to exotic animals that have been removed from their natural habitats? If they're lucky, they'll be sent—along with more familiar animals such as cats and dogs—to join John Bergmann at the Popcorn Park Zoo in New Jersey.*

Difference Maker: John Bergmann and Popcorn Park

Newspaper Article By David Karas

CLOSE READ Notes

1. **READ ▶** As you read lines 1–48, begin to cite text evidence.
   - Underline quotes that reveal Bergmann's character, and explain in the margin what aspects of his character are shown.
   - Circle how Bergmann treats the animals and how they respond to him.

"The chickens crawl all over the office, and they lay eggs on my desk," says John Bergmann, who chuckles as he lifts up the towels that cover the papers in his office—which is in a barn. "It's all part of the job, I guess."

Mr. Bergmann is general manager of Popcorn Park, a federally licensed zoo nestled in the Pinelands of southern New Jersey that caters to distressed wildlife and exotic and domesticated animals. Part of the statewide Associated Humane Societies, the zoo cares for thousands of animals each year, including those that are ill, injured, exploited, abused, or older.

"Animals find their way to us," he says. "This all happened by accident."

The zoo began in 1977 as a pet adoption center when staff started receiving calls about distressed wildlife, including a raccoon that had been injured when it got caught in a trap.

CLOSE READ
Notes

As new animals came in, more cages were built, and piece by piece the zoo was born.

Today, more than 200 animals call the zoo home—including African lions, tigers, mountain lions, a camel, emus, wallabies, monkeys, bears, and, of course, the peacocks that roam the property and greet the more than 75,000 annual visitors in the parking lot.

On a recent morning, Bergmann made his rounds to the different cages, greeting the animals individually and calling them by name.

The routine is a familiar one for the animal residents, who treat Bergmann like a rock star. Chickens hitch a ride on the back of his golf cart, and tigers twice his size rise to greet him and gain his attention.

"You are around [the animals] a lot," he says of his occupation. "I guess there is some realization [by them] that you have done something for them."

Bergmann has bonded with each of the animals in his care, but Bengali is a special case. The Bengal tiger came to the zoo from Texas, where he had been rescued from an abusive, neglectful environment.

emaciated:

"He was **emaciated** . . . you could see all his ribs and bones," Bergmann recalls. "The way he looked, it was like he didn't have a will to live."

The staff slowly nursed Bengali back to health. He underwent surgeries to repair broken teeth and other ailments. His largest challenge, though, was getting back up to his proper weight—400 pounds—from 180 pounds.

It was when Bengali met an old lioness in the shelter next to his, Bergmann says, that he truly began to come alive. Each day, Bengali

walked the fence to catch a glimpse of his new friend, until he finally built up the energy to walk his entire habitat.

"When he went out, he saw her, and he just got so excited," Bergmann said, smiling.

Today, when Bergmann visits, the massive tiger **chuffs** at him—a greeting—and rubs against the fence.

chuff:

But helping animals recover from conditions like this isn't achieved by sticking to an eight-hour workday.

"It is sometimes a 24/7 job," Bergmann says. "Dante [a tiger] is feeling uncomfortable, [so] you stay here through the night."

Dante, much the opposite of Bengali, became afraid of a lioness in a neighboring cage after his companion died. It took many nights of comfort and coaxing to help him again become comfortable with his enclosure.

Bergmann credits his family with accommodating his unpredictable schedule—and his habit of occasionally bringing animals home with him to give them a little extra care and attention.

2. **◀ REREAD** Reread lines 31–48. Why does Karas include the story of Bengali? Support your answer with explicit textual evidence.

3. **READ ▶** As you read lines 49–90, continue to cite textual evidence.

- Write two examples in the margin of how the zoo resembles a family, and underline sentences that support your answer.
- Circle how animals become residents of Popcorn Park.

CLOSE READ
Notes

"My whole family has grown up with this," he says. His son, a veterinarian, works at the zoo, and his daughter, a teacher, uses animal themes in her lesson plans.

At the end of the day, Bergmann considers himself lucky.

"A lot of times you work seven days a week, and you don't even know it," he says. "You are doing what you love. You enjoy helping the animals out."

The staff has seen a wide range of animals find their way to Popcorn Park.

Porthos, a lion, was found in a converted horse stall with the floor caked with excrement. Doe, a deer, is so old she has gray eyelashes. And Princess, a camel, has a talent for picking the winner of sporting events.

"We take them when no one else wants them," Bergmann says, admitting that the zoo can sometimes resemble a retirement home for older creatures living out their senior years in peace.

The zoo also has a large kennel, which has high adoption rates for the household pets there. Many come from states with severely overcrowded animal shelters, where animals would not be held long before being put down.

The zoo runs primarily on donations, Bergmann says, which help offset the cost of its 42 staff members, including veterinarians and animal control officers, who provide constant care for the animals.

And that doesn't include supplies and specialty food items needed to accommodate the picky eaters among the menagerie.

On a recent afternoon, the aroma of homemade mashed potatoes filled the zoo's kitchen. The meal was for one of the animals that enjoyed variety at lunchtime.

And, honoring the zoo's namesake, visitors can purchase air-popped popcorn to share with some of the farm and domesticated animals that have less-rigid diets.

4. **REREAD AND DISCUSS** Reread lines 57–90. In a small group, discuss the ways Popcorn Park is different from other zoos.

5. **READ** As you read lines 91–119, continue to cite textual evidence.

- Underline what Bergmann wants people to learn from the zoo.
- Circle examples of Bergmann's compassionate character.

> *He didn't belong here. . . . All we did was keep him company when he was here.*

Beyond helping animals in need, Bergmann says that the zoo has a larger mission.

"I always hope, and I always think, [that visitors] walk out of here with more compassion for animals than they walked in here with," he says. "I always thought that was a [large part] of our mission, that we would change the minds of people to have more compassion for animals."

While he seems to have found his dream job, Bergmann says he has trouble with one aspect of his work: saying goodbye to the animals that die.

Sonny, an elephant, had been brought to the United States from Zimbabwe to be trained for circus work. After he resisted his training, he was sent to a New Mexico zoo, from which he escaped several times.

Rather than putting him down, in 1989 the zoo sent a letter to other facilities across the country to see if anyone might give a new home to the troubled creature.

"We were the only one that raised our hand," Bergmann says.

It took extensive care and much training, but Sonny finally adapted to his new surroundings at Popcorn Park and lived there a dozen more years, dying in 2001.

A local funeral home donated its services to host a ceremony for Sonny, and Bergmann delivered a eulogy.

"He didn't belong here," he said, remembering his friend. "All we did was keep him company when he was here."

For Bergmann, it was bittersweet to see Sonny leave Popcorn Park. "It is very sad that he is not with us any longer," Bergmann says, holding back tears as he adds a comforting thought. "But he is with his herd again."

6. REREAD Reread lines 116–119. What does Bergmann mean when he says that Sonny is "with his herd again"?

SHORT RESPONSE

Cite Text Evidence What is the author's purpose in writing this newspaper article? How does Karas portray Bergmann? Review your reading notes, and be sure to **cite text evidence** in your response.

Acknowledgments

"Arachne" from *Greek Myths* by Olivia E. Coolidge. Text copyright © 1949, renewed © 1977 by Olivia E. Coolidge. Reprinted by permission of Houghton Mifflin Harcourt Publishing Company.

"The Arch Hunters" excerpted and titled from "The Hidden Southwest: The Arch Hunters" by James Vlahos from *adventure.nationalgeographic.com.* Text copyright © 2008 by James Vlahos. Reprinted by permission of James Vlahos.

"Big Things Come in Small Packages" from *Don't Split the Pole: Tales of Down-Home Folk Wisdom* by Eleanora E. Tate. Text copyright © 1997 by Eleanora E. Tate. Reprinted by permission of Eleanora E. Tate.

Excerpt from *A Christmas Carol: Scrooge and Marley* by Israel Horovitz. Text copyright © 1979 by Israel Horovitz. Reprinted by permission of William Morris Endeavor Entertainment, LLC.

"Difference Maker: John Bergman and Popcorn Park" (retitled from "John Bergman runs a special zoo for older, exploited, and abused animals") by David Karas, October 25, 2012 from *www.csmonitor.com.* Text copyright © by David Karas. Reprinted by permission of David Karas.

Excerpt from "Doris Is Coming" from *Drinking Coffee Elsewhere* by ZZ Packer. Text copyright © 2003 by ZZ Packer. Reprinted by permission of Canongate Books Ltd., Riverhead Books, an imprint of Penguin Group (USA) Inc., and Highbridge Audio.

"Heartbeat" by David Yoo. Text copyright © 2005 by David Yoo. Reprinted by permission of Writers House, LLC, on behalf of David Yoo.

"He-y Come On O-ut" by Shinichi Hoshi from *The Best Japanese Science Fiction Stories.* Text copyright © 1989 by Shinichi Hoshi. Reprinted by permission of Barricade Books.

Excerpt by Joan Vernikos from the compilation of "Is Space Exploration Worth the Cost?" by Stephen Dubner from *www.freakonomics.com,* January 11, 2008. Text copyright © by Joan Vernikos. Reprinted by permission of Joan Vernikos.

Excerpt from "The Most Daring of Our Leaders" from *Freedom's Daughters: The Unsung Heroines of the Civil Rights Movement from 1830 to 1970* by Lynne Olson. Text copyright © 2001 by Lynne Olson. Reprinted by permission of Scribner, a division of Simon & Schuster, Inc., and Lichtman, Singer, Trister & Ross.

Excerpt from *Polar Dream* by Helen Thayer. Text copyright © 1993 by Helen Thayer. Reprinted by permission of Helen Thayer.

"Prayer to the Pacific" from *Storyteller* by Leslie Marmon Silko. Text copyright © 1981, 2012 by Leslie Marmon Silko. Reprinted by permission of Viking Penguin, a division of Penguin Group (USA) Inc., and Wylie Agency LLC.

"Problems with Hurricanes" from *Maraca: New and Selected Poems 1965-2000* by Victor Hernández Cruz. Text copyright © 1991 by Victor Hernández Cruz. Reprinted by permission of The Permissions Company on behalf of Coffee House Press.

Excerpt from *Stan Lee Presents A Christmas Carol by Charles Dickens* by Marvel. Text copyright © 2007 by Marvel. Adapted from the classic novel by Charles Dickens. Reprinted by permission of Marvel Entertainment.

"Stinging Tentacles Offer Hint of Oceans' Decline" by Elisabeth Rosenthal from *The New York Times,* August 3, 2008. Text copyright © 2008 by The New York Times. Reprinted by permission of PARS International on behalf of The New York Times. All rights reserved.

"Tornado at Talladega" from *Blacks* by Gwendolyn Brooks. Text copyright © 1945, 1949, 1953, 1960, 1963, 1968, 1969, 1970, 1971, 1975, 1981, 1987 by Gwendolyn Brooks. Reprinted by permission of Brooks Permissions.

Index of Titles & Authors